MW01068855

THE BOOK OF DHARMA
MAKING ENLIGHTENED CHOICES

THE
BOOK *of*
DHARMA

MAKING ENLIGHTENED CHOICES

SIMON HAAS

VEDA WISDOM BOOKS

Readers interested in the subject matter of this book
are invited to correspond with the author at
simon@bookofdharma.com

Published by Veda Wisdom Books
an imprint of The English Word Factory
www.englishwordfactory.com

© Simon Haas 2013
The moral right of the author has been asserted

All rights reserved
No part of this publication may be reproduced, stored in a
retrieval system, or transmitted in any form or by any means,
without the prior permission in writing of the publisher,
nor be otherwise circulated in any form of binding or cover
other than that in which it is published and without a similar
condition including this condition being imposed on the
subsequent purchaser

Veda Wisdom Books is committed to a sustainable future.
All our books are printed on at least partly recycled or
sustainable paper.

VEDA WISDOM BOOKS

First published in Great Britain
First edition, 2013

ISBN 978-0-9575185-0-6

"THE PURPOSE OF
PROCLAIMING DHARMA
IS TO ENHANCE THE POTENCY
OF BEINGS."

– *Mahabharata,*
Shanti-parva ("The Book of Peace")

Contents

Part II
THE FOUR DHARMA PRINCIPLES

Part III
APPLYING THE DHARMA CODE IN EVERYDAY LIFE

THE VOICE OF AN OLD INTELLIGENCE

WHEN I WAS A YOUNG BOY, I wanted to be an archaeologist. I read about the discovery of the ancient cities of Troy, Tiryns and Mycenae, previously thought to be simply fictitious. I dreamed of excavating the legendary golden city of Dwarka, said to have been lost under the Arabian Sea, off the coast of India. I began to learn Sanskrit, one of the oldest surviving languages in the world, and to study texts whose origin, leading chronologists admit, still remains shrouded in mystery.[1] I also took up Archaeology, and began working at excavations. I was thirteen years old.

Long before the rise of the first Babylonian dynasty of kings in about 1830 BCE, a great civilization flourished in what is today known as India.[2] From remote antiquity to modern times, descriptions of India's fabulous riches have fired the ambitions of travellers and kings. The part of India known as Malabar, Marco Polo recounted in the thirteenth century, was "the noblest and richest country in the world."[3] By then Marco Polo had seen many lands, not least China.

It is these descriptions that drove Christopher Columbus to set sail across the Atlantic on 3 August 1492 in the hope of discovering a passage to India. The Sanskrit texts themselves speak of powerful empires that emerged from an ancient and forgotten world. If there was anything true and tangible about these old legends, I hoped to help unearth it.

But over the years that followed, my study of thousands of Sanskrit passages led me to something far more significant: the power of inward-looking perception. The texts kept alluding to it, referring to a secret living knowledge.[4] Formerly the reserve of mystics and philosopher-kings, this knowledge is said to surpass the greatest treasury. It is a knowledge of the higher self that vanquishes fear, lamentation and confusion – the three types of suffering associated with time.[5] Fear is suffering associated with the future, lamentation with the past, and confusion with the present. The power of inward-looking perception is said to conquer all three and to lift one to a higher state of being, a powerful state of inner freedom. It gives a person the ability to shape his or her world.

My study of the ancient Sanskrit texts eventually took me to a number of temple monasteries in India, where I lived for nearly ten years altogether. With the help of the temple priests, I began studying the medieval manuscripts in some of the temple libraries. I slept on the floor with the other monks, only a thin straw mat between me and the cold stone. I also shaved my head like the other monks. It was a simple life. There was no heating, warm water, washing machine, TV, radio or other form of comfort or amenity.

Every day, we would rise at 4am. I would sweep and mop the temple courtyard, and then continue with my studies. Could the ancient and guarded wisdom of the East help us overcome our contemporary everyday problems in the West? It seemed possible. I applied myself diligently, eager to understand the essence of the ancient teachings within a living tradition. Gradually, my interest in digging up forgotten ruins or retrieving lost artefacts from the seabed dwindled. I began developing a new focus in life: the archaeology, or uncovering, of ancient wisdom.

During this time, I started apprenticing with a 73-year-old master, from an unbroken line of teachers and students going back thousands of years. By "master", I mean someone who has mastered the mind. My teacher, I observed, was not besieged by the disabling forces of anxiety, unease and dissatisfaction. I lived and travelled with this wise, unassuming master, who became like a father to me. I began to learn from him the hidden meaning of the Sanskrit codes. This was the breakthrough I had been looking for. I realized I had been approaching these texts in the wrong way. While I was looking at them for *information*, they were designed to lead me to *transformation*. The texts were just signposts that pointed the way to a deeper way of seeing.[6]

I now know that the power of inward-looking perception is very real. This wisdom lies hidden, but it has not been lost. I sometimes wonder if it isn't one of the world's most valuable, and oddly enduring, secrets. The Sanskrit texts refer to it as "the secret knowledge of kings".[7]

⚜ UNCOVERING AN ANCIENT WISDOM ⚜

Rich in gems, silks, spices and gold, India became the target of twenty-six different invasions. Semiramis, Queen of Assyria, sent an army into India twenty-two centuries before Christ. She was followed by Cyrus of Persia in 530 BCE, and then by more fabled conquerors like Alexander the Great, Genghis Khan, Tamerlane and Nadir Shah, who plundered the land and withdrew with loot and lore.

This wisdom intended for kings was therefore deliberately concealed. The brahmins jealously guarded their secret. Encoded in sacred Sanskrit texts, it continued to be passed down in secrecy from master to student in an unbroken succession for generations. In this way, the wisdom of the elders was kept alive, like a temple fire that is never allowed to die out but that burns on for centuries.

This book "excavates" part of these teachings from India's cradle of wisdom. It focuses on the wisdom of Dharma – a system for making powerful choices, designed to reverse our habit of inferiority to our full potential. That system remains just as highly effective today as it was in a bygone age, when it taught emperors the art of ruling skilfully.

The oldest texts of India were passed down from one generation to the next in a highly sophisticated oral tradition long before they were ever written down. Composed millennia ago, the Vedic and Puranic texts are therefore the echo of a different epoch, of a forgotten world. Their wisdom is often buried in religious rites and hymns, obscured by Sanskrit terminology, or concealed in stories and allegories. This in itself makes the texts difficult to access. Thus, their secrets continue to remain intact, their powerful essence concealed.

The purpose of this book is to present a cultural translation of the teachings of Dharma, bringing them alive. This book is therefore an unlocking of ancient texts for contemporary readers.

I have great confidence in the teachings of Dharma. My own life began with many tragedies. My mother was a heroin addict, who spent the first years of my life flitting in and out of prison. She died when I was young. My father, meanwhile, was for understandable reasons fairly absent as a parent. That these and many other challenges have not left an indelible mark on me is thanks to the inestimable power of the teachings of Dharma that I have tried to apply in my life. Dharma can transform a person. It can alter her way of seeing for the better. This is why I would like to share these particular teachings first of all.

The ancient texts of India contain many layers of instructions, some more esoteric than others. The teachings of Dharma presented in this book are potent, but they are also not the most confidential. There remains much more.

⸙ A FEW WORDS ABOUT THIS BOOK ⸙

This book does not pretend to offer any quick fix or easy recipe for resolving life's thorny challenges. Rather, this is a book of principles. Success depends on the extent we actually *apply* these principles in our life – which requires personal effort, patience and practice.

If you sit on a bicycle with your hands on the handlebar, your act of steering has no potency or effect unless you are moving forward.[8] Similarly, these wisdom principles are principles *in action*. We invoke them by living them. When we no longer live them, they withdraw. They remain then on the level of artefacts of the mind, what the ancients describe as "mere weariness of the tongue".[9]

Embodying wisdom in our everyday life is the hardest thing to do. We cannot *buy* "living wisdom", in the way we might purchase a university education or a hairdryer. Even academic study will not yield the desired result. If it were that easy, we would all be purchasing our own personal transformation at the shopping mall and become "enlightened masters". The teachings in this book are therefore more like a map. The journey itself is one only we can take; and it may well be a journey that takes us a lifetime.

Some exotic lands have mines of sapphires and diamonds. Others are rich in silver or gold. Some, like India, have hidden treasure troves of wisdom. The sages of India believed, however, that there is only one wisdom in this world, which does not belong to any single nation or culture.[10] That wisdom came to be known as the *philosophia perennis* – universal truths that transcend time and space.[11] We can discover that wisdom, or at least fragments of it, in all civilizations and traditions. To emphasize the universal quality of the teachings of Dharma, I have therefore deliberately drawn on the insights of writers and poets from other traditions and periods, who elegantly expressed the essence of these teachings.

⚘ THE ANCIENT ART OF LIVING SKILFULLY ⚘

The sages and mystics of India searched for the magnificence that lies hidden to the human eye. They considered this inner territory to be more valuable than the outer. In their quest, they discovered the path of Dharma, or the art of bringing out our full latent potential as human beings.

In an environment that is becoming increasingly complex, it's helpful to have a set of deeper principles to help us make decisions that we can be confident will lead to optimal outcomes. This is what the Dharma teachings are designed to offer us.

Wisdom reveals itself through action; but wise action requires the making of wise choices. Wisdom is therefore no less than the art of making good choices.

We spend a lot of time and energy in our life trying to improve our skills, but little time trying to improve our choices. Our character is reflected not in the gifts we are endowed with at birth or the skills we improve, but in the choices we make over the course of a lifetime. As Jeff Bezos, founder and CEO of Amazon, pointed out:

> I will hazard a prediction: when you are eighty years old and, in a quiet moment of reflection, narrating for only yourself the most personal version of your life story, the telling that will be most compact and meaningful will be the series of choices you have made. In the end, we are our choices.[12]

This book is about the art of making powerful choices. It is about living our life skilfully, rather than haphazardly.

Notes

1. For instance, see Moriz Winternitz, *A History of Indian Literature*, Vol. 1 (1927), p. 24. Most Indologists agree that the Vedic texts were passed down from generation to generation in an oral tradition long before they were put in writing. According to Winternitz, "Vedic literature extends from an unknown past (say x) to 500 BC" (Ruth Reyna, *Introduction to Indian Philosophy* [1964], p. 16).

2. There is archaeological evidence of cities in the Indus Valley dating as far back as at least 3300 BCE. This is more than 1,400 years before the rise of the first Babylonian dynasty of kings.

3. Marco Polo, *The Travels of Marco Polo, a Venetian, in the Thirteenth Century* (1818), p. 624.

4. For example, see *Bhagavad-gita*, 9.1 and 9.2; and *Bhagavata Purana*, 1.1.8, 2.9.31 and 12.12.4. The qualifier "living" is implied, but is especially apt for an accurate rendering of the Sanskrit word *vijnana*. It is a "living knowledge" in that it is intended to be lived, or embodied in a person. This is how it is kept alive. *Vijnana* – in contradistinction to *jnana* – is experiential and transformative, rather than merely theoretical or informative. As such, this knowledge was passed down from teacher to student in a living tradition, and students were required to embody it in their lives to be eligible to pass it on.

5. According to the *Bhagavata Purana*, the wisdom of India is designed to free one from fear, lamentation and bewilderment. For instance, see *Bhagavata Purana*, 1.7.7.

6. In India, complete understanding of knowledge is referred to as *darshana*, or its "perception" (e.g. *Bhagavad-gita*, 4.34). The ancient texts distinguish between mere theoretical knowledge and transformative wisdom, which is perceptual (e.g. *Bhagavad-gita*, 6.8 and 9.1–9.2).

7. For example, *Bhagavad-gita*, 9.2. See commentaries by Shri Ramanujacharya and Shri Baladeva Vidyabhushana, as well as Angelika Malinar, *The Bhagavadgita: Doctrines and Contexts* (2007), p. 147. According to Malinar, it is a knowledge of kings (*raja-vidya*), guarded by kings (*raja-guhya*), and accessible through perception (*pratyaksa-avagama*). The teachings of the *Bhagavad-gita*, a classic Dharma text, were passed down in a succession of kings. The ancient Dharma texts of India refer repeatedly to great "philosopher-kings" or "seer-kings" (*raja-rishis*). For instance, see *Bhagavad-gita*, 4.2 and 9.33, and *Bhagavata Purana*, 8.24.55.

8. Thanks to Bert Mulder, associate professor at The Hague University, for this apt metaphor.

9. For example, the *Brihad-aranyaka Upanishad* (4.4.21) distinguishes between perfect knowledge (*prajna*), which manifests in action, and the knowledge of books, which it describes as "mere weariness of the tongue".

10. The *Rig Veda*, for instance, states, "Truth is one, though the learned speak of it in many ways" (1.164.46). The *Bhagavata Purana* similarly advises (11.8.10), "As the honey-bee extracts nectar from all flowers, big and small, a discriminating person should take the essence from all sacred texts."

11. The idea of a perennial philosophy (Latin: *philosophia perennis*, "eternal philosophy") has great antiquity, and can be found in many of the world's religions and philosophies. The term *philosophia perennis* appears to have been first used by Agostino Steuco, to title a treatise, *De perenni philosophia libri X*, published in 1540.

12. Jeff Bezos, Princeton University graduation address (May 2010).

I

LIVING BY INTELLIGENT DESIGN

CHAPTER 1

THE UNDISCOVERED SELF

THINK BACK. What we remember most clearly about our life are our successes and our failures, the times of excellence and of foolishness. By engaging with the world, we generate a set of outcomes in our life. These outcomes are no accident: they reflect the quality of our choices.

We are continually making choices. Our choices are only ever as good as our state of being when we make them. If we are confused, our choices will necessarily be confused. If we are inspired, our choices will be inspired also.

In ancient India, the sages, known as Rishis, could understand that we are beings of great potency – which we demonstrate through occasional flashes of magnificence. But we lose ourselves in a small human story. We fall into habits of inferiority to our full potential. By acting from this inferior position, we experience inferior results.

Optimal choices require an optimal state of being. The Rishis therefore developed methods for awakening the higher self, so we can inhabit a space of formidable strength.

This knowledge was deemed especially important for kings. The actions of a king or queen will affect thousands, perhaps even millions, of people. It was essential, therefore, that a monarch had the highest quality of thoughts, words and actions. This need gave rise to a lore for kings. Chapter 1 will explain how those teachings for kings from the past can help us surmount the challenges of life in the present.

⚹ MANIFESTING DHARMA ⚹

Before the Wright Brothers' historic first flight in 1903, they tested two-hundred different wing designs. Their first attempts to create a "flying machine" suffered repeated failures. But through patience and dedication they discovered that with the right design, two large and heavy metal appendages can suddenly produce something remarkable: lift. They can become wings. A contraption too heavy to lift manually suddenly soars into the sky, carrying a human passenger.

We experience the phenomenon of "lift" in our everyday life also. Some ways of thinking and acting drag us down, while others uplift us and lead to optimal outcomes. Dharma is what we might call the phenomenon of "lift" in life, when our state of being is elevated, and our thoughts, words and actions come from the very best place within us. To manifest Dharma is to live in accord with the hidden laws of life – akin to the principles of flight in aeronautics.

The word "Dharma" actually comes from the Sanskrit for "to uphold, support or sustain".[13] We all have some experience of Dharma. When Dharma is present, it feels as if we are acting in complete accord with the universe. It is as if a powerful unseen force is sustaining our efforts, endowing them with potency. To invoke Dharma is to manifest excellence through "right action" – action that leads to optimal outcomes. This results in the unfolding of our potential. Dharma, which is something highly experiential, brings about the full flourishing of a human being.

Thousands of years ago, the Rishis formulated the Dharma Code, a technology for manifesting Dharma in our everyday life. We can call the Dharma Code a set of "power principles", because these principles awaken the higher self, the seat of inborn power. In doing so, they help us create the best possible perceptual world. When applied to any system, the Dharma Code acts as a set of optimal design principles.

⚡ INSTRUCTIONS FOR RULING WISELY ⚡

Many readers will have already come across teachings intended for monarchs. One of the most widely read such texts is *The Art of War*, composed some 2,500 years ago by Sun Tzu for the King of Wu.[14] Also well-known is Niccolò Machiavelli's *The Prince*, which he dedicated to the grandson of the de facto ruler of the Florentine Republic.[15]

Much of the knowledge in the ancient texts of India was intended primarily for emperors and rulers too. It was previously taught to great philosopher-kings, or "Dharma kings", in an unbroken succession of enlightened masters going back thousands of years.[16] Thus, the *Bhagavad-gita*, a leading Dharma text, speaks of a "knowledge for kings, guarded by kings".[17]

The Art of War and *The Prince* have become renowned; but the teachings for Dharma kings from India have not yet been presented in a cogent, accessible way. As a system, they therefore remain to this day largely undiscovered. This is surprising given that the Dharma kings possessed unearthly integrity and valour, and reigned over what were previously the most prosperous territories on earth.

Now, the reader may be wondering, "If this knowledge is meant specifically for kings, how relevant can it be to me, a regular person without a kingdom?" However, we are actually far more like kings and queens than we may realize. As the reader will soon discover, we are immensely powerful beings, with the ability to shape our perceptual world. We each have a kingdom. That kingdom is our life, or the world as we perceive it. We have the ability to determine the quality of that world. Whether we are fully aware of it or not, and whether we like it or not, we are each a sovereign already. The first step to creating the life we want for ourselves is to acknowledge who we are, and to take responsibility for the state of our kingdom.

The quality of our kingdom, or of our life, will necessarily reflect the quality with which we rule. We want our life to be extraordinary, but we forget that our life will only ever be as good as the design principles we use to create it. To have a flourishing life, we need to search for the wisdom that will allow us to rule wisely, or skilfully. This is where the Dharma teachings come in.

There are many kinds of "kingdoms" to which we can apply the teachings of Dharma. Our kingdom can be whatever we choose it to be – whatever we have some dominion or influence over. If we are running a company, our company is our kingdom. Otherwise, if we are heading a team or working on a specific project, that team or project is a kingdom. The principles of Dharma will apply to any kingdom we choose. This is one reason they are so useful.

Our most important kingdom, however, is always the territory of our personal life. Indeed, this ancient system must necessarily *begin* with that territory. How is it possible for a person to lead others in any capacity, let alone govern a nation, if she has not yet mastered the territory within? Everything is contained within this primary kingdom. Mastery of life ensures mastery of all else.

In India, it was not sufficient for a monarch to rule by virtue of blood line alone: from a young age a ruler-to-be had to master the teachings of Dharma. That meant learning to overcome fear, lamentation and confusion. Such mastery awakens our inborn power. It is to inhabit "a state of wholeness, even though your body may be broken; a state of riches, even though you may have no earthly possessions; a state of imperturbable peace and quietude, even though the world around you may go up in flames."[18]

We cannot escape action – not even for a moment. Even when we decide not to act, we are engaged in a form of action. What we can do, however, is learn how to act *skilfully*. This entails making skilful choices. We are engaged in an ongoing process of making choices. What is life but a continual dynamic of accepting and rejecting, of saying "yes" or "no". That simple process guides the direction of our life. It creates our world. Everything depends upon the quality of our state of mind when we engage in this process, at any given moment. The philosopher-kings and queens of the past understood that the quality of their thinking had the potency to shape their perceptual world. Therefore, they ceaselessly endeavoured to find and develop the best in themselves.

⚹ AWAKENING THE HIGHER SELF ⚹

Many people identify with their physical body. But the body is simply a covering of the self, like a garment. It is the vehicle by which we, consciousness, express ourselves in this world. The eye does not see, the ear does not hear, and the flesh does not feel. It is consciousness that sees, hears and feels. When consciousness leaves the body, the body is inactive, like a vehicle without a driver.

When we look at photos of our childhood, it is fairly easy to recognize how we are distinct from the changing physical body. We are the life force that animates that body. When people identify too closely with the body, they think strongly in terms of body distinctions such as black and white, male and female, fat and thin, Indian and American. But all these designations refer to the body only.

Consciousness, which animates the body, shines through the lens of the thinking mind. While it's fairly easy to understand we are not the body, it's a little more difficult to understand that we exist even beyond the creations of our mind. This becomes more evident to those who meditate, which is a practice for stilling the restless mind. Consciousness does not require thinking; but thinking requires consciousness. This tells us that we, the self, exist at a deeper level even than thinking.

The mind produces a continuous stream of conversation, or mental noise. Much of what the mind has to say is repetitive and fairly unhelpful. The mind worries about the future, laments about the past, and generates confusion in the present. When consciousness finds even a little release from the oppressive constraints of the mind, human beings achieve a level of freedom and potency that is quite remarkable.[19] In this book, I will refer to this as the awakening of the "higher self", or the Dharma king or queen within us.[20]

We all have experience of higher and lower qualities within us. We are capable of astonishing small-mindedness and folly, as well as of surprising courage and wisdom. The mind can elevate or degrade us. The Dharma king or queen arises when we act in a way that expresses the best in ourselves. This occurs when the mind works to help rather than to hinder us. From time to time we experience this state. Sometimes, for instance, the higher self is stirred by adversity, when a situation calls on us to muster everything we are capable of to deal with a tragedy or help a loved one. Casting aside self-doubt, anxiety, self-pity and other obstacles generated by the mind, we suddenly find ourselves accomplishing extraordinary things. These experiences are valuable: they are windows that reveal what is possible for us.

Before we explore ways of deliberately awakening the higher self and manifesting Dharma in our life, we will take a closer look at the Dharma king or queen's most important territory – our perceptual world. Thus, we will now explore the underlying "architecture" of our world, as well as the three laws of perception that govern it.

Notes

13. The Sanskrit word "Dharma" first appears in the ancient *Rig Veda*, as *dhárman* (63 usages), denoting a thing that upholds or supports – or, more simply, a "foundation". Borrowed heavily over time to denote a variety of ideas, the word straddles a complex set of meanings and interpretations. In Buddhism, for instance, Dharma generally refers to the teachings of the Buddha and those who have elaborated on those teachings. In this book, I am using "Dharma" in a very specific way, in referring to the awakening of our full latent potential through "right action".

14. At the close of the Han period, the Great Ts'ao Ts'ao wrote a short preface for his edition of Sun Tzu. He states therein that the thirteen chapters of the book were composed specifically for King Ho Lu, ruler of the Wu State. This is supported by the internal evidence of section I.15, in which it seems clear that some ruler is addressed.

15. Niccolò Machiavelli dedicated *The Prince* to Lorenzo di Piero de' Medici, a member of the ruling Florentine Medici family and the grandson of "Lorenzo the Magnificent", the de facto ruler of the Florentine Republic during the Italian Renaissance.

16. For example, see *Bhagavad-gita*, 4.2. The ancient texts of India refer to great "philosopher-kings" or "seer-kings" (*raja-rishis*) – e.g. *Ramayana, Mahabharata, Bhagavata Purana* (at least 66 references).

17. *Bhagavad-gita*, 9.2. See commentary by Shri Ramanujacharya, as well as Angelika Malinar, *The Bhagavadgita: Doctrines and Contexts* (2007), pp. 144–50, 225 and 232. According to Malinar, it is a knowledge of kings (*raja-vidya*), guarded by kings (*raja-guhya*), and accessible through perception (*pratyaksa-avagama*).

18. Nisargadatta Maharaj and Robert Powell, *The Nectar of Immortality: Sri Nisargadatta Maharaj's Discourses on the Eternal* (2004), p. xv.

19. See *Bhagavata Purana*, 12.4.33: "When a cloud, which is created by the sun, is torn apart, the eye can see the true form of the sun. Likewise, when the self destroys her covering of the ego by inquiry, she regains her true awareness."

20. The *Bhagavad-gita* sets out the qualities of the higher self in Chapter 16, describing them as "god-like" or "divine" (*sampadam daivim*). This chapter also provides a detailed description of the lower qualities of humans in terms that are remarkably fitting today, millennia after this text was composed.

CHAPTER 2

Three Laws of Perception

Humans have climbed 29,000 feet to the top of Mount Everest, the highest place on earth. They have descended 35,800 feet to the deepest place on earth, the bottom of Mariana Trench in the Pacific Ocean. They have journeyed into the infinite void of outer space, and sent a space probe to fly by Pluto and its moons, Charon, Nix and Hydra. In our personal life, we also continually try to push back our frontiers. But there remains always one frontier so close to us that we rarely think to cross far beyond it.

When we look for new experiences, we are in the habit of reaching out into the world; but few ever turn in the opposite direction to explore the vast territory within them. Thus, when we travel to another city or country, we rarely venture far from where we truly are, our familiar state of being. Whatever we see and hear and smell, we interpret through our existing perspective. If we are troubled by something, we take our troubles with us. In the end, wherever we go, we only encounter ourselves.

Our greatest journeys are therefore not physical, but those that occur within us – as when we experience a profound shift in perception, or when some of the limits of our ordinary perception fall away. Thus, the real voyage of discovery consists not in seeking new landscapes, but in having new eyes.[21] Exploring another country or lifestyle is valuable only when it leads to some inner enlargement. The real aim of any voyage is to look more deeply at ourselves.

In this chapter, we will explore our own perceptual world, by far the most important "kingdom" we each have inherited. We will see how this is largely a kingdom of our own creation. Understanding this kingdom at a deeper level will help the reader better understand the Dharma Code, as well as how to apply it.

⋇ THE SELF AND ITS PERCEPTUAL WORLD ⋇

The texts of India describe the self as "self-luminous".[22] This is because consciousness shines by its own light and illumines the world. We, the light of consciousness, are brighter than the sun and all the stars; for without that inner light of perception, our perceptual world would be filled with ineffable darkness. The self is the light of lights.

We exist at the heart of our perceptual universe. We don't observe our universe because it exists; our universe exists because we are observing it. If you erase the conscious observer, all that remains is energy in flux, devoid of meaning or sense. It is we who give sense and purpose to our universe. We decide whether something is valuable or not, significant or not. We create order and meaning in our world through the words and ideas we have inherited and learned to use, which are simply free creations of the mind. We colour our world with our attitudes and prejudices. The world we know and are so familiar with is, ultimately, a world of our own making.

We each inhabit distinct worlds. What I perceive in my world will differ from what someone else perceives in theirs. When my perceptual world begins to shrink and collapse with old age, theirs may still be expanding with the vitality and confidence of youth. When mine is filled with suffering or pain, theirs may be brimming with happiness and abundance; when mine is a desolate wasteland, theirs may be a fertile valley of opportunity and hope.

Two people can look at the exact same thing and see something totally different. This is because the world we experience is not the only world there is. There are many possible worlds. We create ours with every thought, with every act. As anthropologist Clifford Geertz observed, "man is an animal suspended in webs of significance that he himself has spun."[23]

Through perception directed inward, we become aware of the hidden "architecture" of our perceptual universe. We become aware of the vast, hidden realm of possibility beneath the surface of everyday experience and the tremendous power we each have to shape our world. The only world we know is the world we perceive. Therefore, by altering our perception, we alter the world we know.

⊰ THE ARCHITECTURE OF OUR WORLD ⊰

We are not simple observers: we are creators. In *Dhammapada* (literally, "The Path of Dharma"), Buddha therefore explains: "What we are today comes from our thoughts of yesterday, and our present thoughts build our life of tomorrow: our life is the creation of our mind."[24] There are no idle thoughts. With our thoughts we make the world.

We don't really inhabit a world of rocks, trees and other physical objects. Ours is much more a world of insults and praise, friends and competitors, status symbols, losses and gains. These things are all human creations; they exist only because we believe in them. Happiness and distress, like and dislike, desire and fear – these are all products of the mind too. As the texts of India explain, they have no existence outside the mind.[25]

Our perceptual universes, even if distinct, are interconnected. This allows us to interact with each other and have shared experiences. Shared concepts and categories build a consensual reality. We in effect "buy into" a particular version of reality. We agree to a particular set of ground rules, a common history, a basic "way of seeing". But it's important to remember that these ground rules don't exist independently of us. They exist in our world *because* we have assimilated them. By understanding how we construct our perceptual world, we will be able to understand how we can apply the teachings of Dharma to better it.

Human beings can learn to manipulate the elements of

perception – such as our desires, attitudes, purpose and direction of attention – transforming them into powerful tools to alter perception at will. Even a simple awareness of the way they create our world is sufficient to release some of their hold on us.

⚹ LESSONS FROM THE MILLIONAIRE TRAMP ⚹

Born in Boston about the year 1812, James Henry Paine came from one of the most famous of Massachusetts families. His grandfather, Robert Treat Paine, had been one of the signers of the Declaration of Independence. The young James had inherited a sizable fortune, and had carefully invested it to make himself a wealthy millionaire.

Over the years, however, James became increasingly miserly. He hid or invested all his wealth in such a way that no one could find it, and spent his days in New York in squalor and abject poverty. "He would purchase an ounce of tea," *The New York Times* reported in February 1886, "then secure from a restaurant boiling water with which to prepare it, and this, with the bits of stale bread, constituted, so far as was known, his food."[26]

James was recognized within the local community as highly astute, "a man of uncommon intellect". But his appearance and habits were so slovenly that no one ever imagined he had any money. Only the partners of a few exclusive financial firms knew who he was. They called him "the millionaire tramp".

Over time, James's habits of miserliness became still more

extreme. On Christmas Eve of 1885, James was discovered dead in his small, lonely room. He had been knocked down by a truck on Broadway, and was badly hurt. After having had his broken leg set, he had refused a doctor for further treatment, insisting he could not afford one. In the end, James was a victim of his own outlook in life.

Unusual cases often provide unusual insight: they help us see what is normally hidden from view. By ordinary accounting standards, James and others like him (there have been quite a few similar reported cases) are millionaires; but in their own perceptual world, they are poor. Their impoverished world is as real to them as our own world is to us.

We adopt our own distinct set of habits and attitudes unconsciously and unquestioningly. Over time they ossify and become more difficult to alter, and also more invisible to us. Those who are able to *choose* their attitude hold great power and inner freedom. They have the potential for extraordinary action. Viktor Frankl, a survivor of Auschwitz and other concentration camps during World War II, describes people like this:

> We who lived in concentration camps can remember the men who walked through the huts comforting others, giving away their last piece of bread. They may have been few in number, but they offer sufficient proof that everything can be taken from a man but one thing: the last of the human freedoms – to choose one's attitude in any given set of circumstances, to choose one's own way.[27]

We each have the ability to create our world. But we have forgotten our potency and are living out a small human story. Much like James Henry Paine, we are sitting on a great hidden wealth, but we act as if we are impoverished. Our forgotten wealth is our ability to live intentionally, to alter the very design of our perceptual world.

⸎ UNDERSTANDING THE FIRST LAW ⸎

The ancient texts of India, such as the *Bhagavata Purana*, explain clearly how the world we perceive emerges from our state of being.[28] Perception is creative. I will refer to this as the First Law of Perception.

When we look out into the world through our outward perception, we think we see the world as it is. Actually, we see it *as we make it*, in a telling self-portrait. If, for example, I see someone ravaged by illness, and my response is fear or disgust, I have not defined the individual before me; I have defined myself. Whenever we see something that unnerves us or provokes in us a visceral response, it tells us about ourselves. It discloses a deeper truth. "Everything that irritates us about others," observed Carl Jung, "can lead us to an understanding of ourselves."[29] We don't see things as they are. No, we see them as we are.

Thus, when we judge, our judgments say more about us than about the person or situation we are judging. We forget, as Paul Valéry put it, "that nothing reveals us, exposes our weaknesses more ingeniously than the attitude of pronouncing upon our fellows."[30] When we judge, we define one person only – ourselves, with all our weaknesses, including the need to judge. If we dislike someone, it is because we recognize something in them that is in us. What is not part of us doesn't disturb us. The way we see the world therefore says volumes about who we are.

The First Law of Perception has important implications. If we create our perceptual world as we live, then by embodying Dharma in our life, we will manifest it in our world. As the texts of India explain, if the ruler of a territory is a Dharma king or queen, then Dharma will also be present throughout the kingdom.[31] The Dharma within us is reflected without. It becomes the organizing principle in the construction of our world.

⚹ THE SECOND LAW OF PERCEPTION ⚹

The texts of India teach that our state of being determines how we perceive the world; and likewise, whatever we repeatedly fix our perception on, we become.[32] In other words, we assume the qualities of what we absorb our heart and mind in. This principle is expressed in an ancient saying, found in several traditions in one form or other, and passed down over generations: "As within, so without. As without, so within."[33] The universe is like a large mirror: the way we look at it is how it looks back at us. This is the Second Law of Perception.

Our state of being is reflected in the world. If we are fearful, what we will see around us are more fearful things. This confirms us in our fear. If we are impatient, what we will see are all those things that frustrate us and try our patience, confirming and sustaining our impatience. If we judge, we will find all the reasons we need to support our judgments. If we ourselves are not at peace, it will not be possible for us to experience peace in our world. This may seem obvious, but we live against the Second Law of Perception almost all the time.

Importantly, if we don't like a reflection, we don't attempt to change it or run away from it. That would be futile. The reflection will simply re-emerge somewhere else. What we need to do is alter what produces that reflection. Similarly, if we don't like our world, it may be unhelpful to focus solely on trying to change it or escape it. We will only find ourselves again. Usually, it is better to turn inward, and first transform what creates that world.

When we move forward in our life without applying the Second Law of Perception, it is a little like looking in the rear-view mirror of a car in an attempt to see in front of us. By looking at the world, we don't find out about the world: we find out about ourselves.

⊰ GNOTHI SEAUTON – "KNOW THYSELF" ⊱

To change our circumstances, we must first change our thinking. To be a millionaire, a person must first stop thinking like a minimum-wage earner. To stop being victimized, a person must first stop thinking like a victim. If we change our mentality, our situation will change; because our situation is the product of our mentality. Ludwig

Wittgenstein put it well:

> If life becomes hard to bear we think of a change in our circumstances. But the most important and effective change, a change in our own attitude, hardly even occurs to us, and the resolution to take such a step is very difficult for us.[34]

People in a dysfunctional relationship often leave their relationship and enter into a new one – only to find themselves trapped in another dysfunctional relationship. Why does this happen time and again? If we simply try to alter the world without altering ourselves, we merely get a different expression of who we are – just another variation of what we are experiencing right now. The way we relate, the way we create our world, doesn't suddenly disappear. We carry it with us wherever we go. This is why lessons will return again and again until, finally, we learn them. The external situation is merely a symptom, an effect.

In ancient Greece, people would travel from distant lands to visit the Oracle of Delphi, bearing gifts and hoping to improve their destiny. As they entered, inscribed high above the entrance of the Temple of Apollo were the words *Gnothi Seauton* – "Know Thyself". Most visitors would probably have passed through that gateway without understanding the real significance of these words. But in them actually lies the answer to whatever question they had travelled so many hundreds of miles to resolve. Real change in life comes about not by altering our outward circumstances, which are merely an effect; it comes about by looking inward and understanding how we have created the very world we now inhabit.

We want our perceptual world to be outstanding; but few stop to consider whether *they* are outstanding. A reflection will never surpass its source. Similarly, our perceptual world will never be better than who we are. Real improvement therefore starts within. Change the landscape within and we reshape the landscape without.

⚡ THE THIRD LAW OF PERCEPTION ⚡

Everything we experience is created in the realm of thought. Situations themselves are neither good nor bad. They don't cause us to experience happiness or distress. Rather, it is our *interpretation* of situations that leads us to experience these things. As the *Bhagavata Purana* explains, "Nothing else but his own mental confusion makes the self experience happiness and distress."[35] Thus, if we can learn to reframe thought, we can begin to alter the world we perceive. By changing our perception, we change our world. This is the Third Law of Perception.

The Rishis of India understood this Third Law and made it the basis of their systems of spiritual practice. The aim of such practice in most traditions of India is to effect personal change by choosing where we place our thoughts, with what kind of attitude, and with what quality of desire or intent. By fixing our heart and mind on something worthy, we are elevated; by fixing it on something unworthy, we are degraded.

Consciousness has great organizing power. But we tend to direct that creative potential outward in the world. We use it to fashion a business or a career. We tend to forget that this creativity, this organizing power, can also be focused inwardly. When directed within, it gives us the ability to transform our world. It takes us out of the box we have created for ourselves, and allows us to choose more freely in an enlarged world.

When our perception is focused outward, in the world of consequences, it is what we may call "surface perception". With this kind of perception, our ability to influence what occurs in our life is extremely limited. We are always reactive: all our actions, even if brilliantly conceived, all emerge from the same patterns of conditioned thought. They are simply different variations of the same underlying desires and attitudes.

When perception is directed inward, however, we become aware of a vast, hidden realm of possibility beneath the surface of everyday experience. This "deep perception" allows us to understand how we construct our world. Through inward-looking perception, we are able to understand the architecture of our perceptual universe. Without inward-looking perception, we remain prisoners of our own thoughts, of our own lack of awareness.

What starts off in the realm of thought ends up soon enough in the realm of purposeful action. The most powerful moment to control what unfolds from our actions is at their very inception, when they are fledgling thoughts. We are each able to be aware of the workings of our thoughts, as a detached observer. This gives us the power to alter thinking, and thereby to create our own reality. Greater than perception of the world is perception of perception.

⚜ DEVELOPING INNER SOVEREIGNTY ⚜

When human beings lose their perceptual ability, they are fairly easy to manipulate. If they prefer not to construct their perceptual universe, someone else will construct it for them. For many years, the media and advertising have filled the gaping void. We live under a continual assault of messages. These messages stir up in us a succession of longings, fears, hopes and prejudices. They dictate who we think we are, what it means to be "successful", what we must acquire, and how we think we ought to feel.

It's a strange irony that while human beings have become adept at influencing the perceptual world of others for their own ends, they retain only the faintest influence over their own perception. We have little control over our own fear, anger, greed, unease, boredom and the other disabling forces that regularly fill our world. What effect can we possibly have on other human beings except to disturb their worlds too?

Therefore, the first step to developing potency is to apply our creative energy inward. Right now, most of us are caught up in many unhelpful habits of thought and behaviour, which weigh us down and lead us to suffering. We have adopted most of these habits without thinking.

In the next chapter, we will look at six of these habits and how they shape the "kingdom" in which we live. When I recognized the extent of such engrained habits in my own life, I understood how little sovereignty I actually have. I always believed I was free and in full control of my life, but I came to realize this is an illusion. My life is being shaped by my unconscious habits, many of which are highly damaging and debilitating. To govern our life means to *choose* the habits we live by.

Notes

21. As Marcel Proust put it, "The only true voyage of discovery, the only really rejuvenating experience, would be not to visit strange lands but to possess other eyes..." Marcel Proust, *Remembrance of Things Past*, Vol. 3 (1982), p. 260.

22. *Bhagavata Purana*, 12.5.8 (*svayam jyotih*).

23. Clifford Geertz, "Thick Description: Toward an Interpretive Theory of Culture", paraphrasing the sociologist Max Weber; in Clifford Geertz (ed.), *The Interpretation of Cultures* (1973), p. 5.

24. Buddha, *Dhammapada*, 1; in J. Mascaro (ed. and trans.), *The Dhammapada* (1973).

25. The *Bhagavata Purana* (11.23.59) affirms, "Nothing else but his own mental confusion makes the self experience happiness and distress." See also *Bhagavata Purana*, 6.15.24 and 12.5.6.

26. "The Millionaire Tramp", *The New York Times*, 20 February 1886.

27. Viktor Emil Frankl, *Man's Search for Meaning* (2004), p. 75.

28. For example, the *Bhagavata Purana* (12.5.6) states, "The physical body, qualities and activities of the self are indeed a product of the mind." See also *Bhagavata Purana*, 6.15.24 and Canto 3, Chapter 26.

29. Carl Gustav Jung, *Memories, Dreams, Reflections* (1989), p. 247.

30. Paul Valéry, *Monsieur Teste* (1947), p. 62.

31. Well-known examples in the Sanskrit literature include the reign of Emperor Yudhisthira, who specifically held the title "Dharma King", and of Shri Rama.

32. What we are is generally referred at as our *adhikara*, which determines what we are able to perceive. A higher *adhikara* permits a higher level of perception. *Sadhana*, or spiritual practice, is a process of fixing our attention on what we wish to become. The principle that we attain what we absorb our hearts and minds in finds clear expression in the *Bhagavata Purana* (7.1.28–29) and *Bhagavad-gita* (8.6).

33. In the Hermetic tradition, for instance, this is the second teaching of alchemy, and is expressed as follows: "As below, so above; and as above, so below." "Below" and "above" refer to the microcosm and the macrocosm, the inner world and the outer world. Legend has it that these teachings of alchemy were also at one time intended to guide kings, and were inscribed in short form on to a single emerald, the "Emerald Tablet", also known as *Tabula Smaragdina*. The Emerald Tablet is a short, cryptic text regarded by European alchemists as the foundation of their art. The oldest documentable source for the text is the *Kitab Sirr al-Asrar* (also known as *Secret of Secrets* or the *Book of the science of government: on the good ordering of statecraft*), a tenth-century compendium of advice for rulers in Arabic, which purports to be a letter from Aristotle to Alexander the Great.

34. Ludwig Wittgenstein, *Culture and Value* (1984), 53e.

35. *Bhagavata Purana*, 11.23.59. Translations from Sanskrit in this book are by the author, unless indicated otherwise.

CHAPTER 3

UNINTELLIGENT DESIGN

L IVING INTENTIONALLY is one of the hardest things to do. Most of us live haphazardly, rather than intentionally. We don't consciously apply any design principles to our life. Instead, we live out inherited patterns of thought and behaviour with limited self-awareness. We forget that the qualities that ennoble us and represent the best in us are not accidental. They are the product of living skilfully.

Designing our life requires a special kind of awareness. We apply design principles in our life all the time – but mostly without awareness. For example, if we believe that our happiness lies in the future, and not in the present moment, that belief is a powerful design principle in our life. It shapes our world. If we battle against time from morning to evening, and never seem to have enough time, our hostile relationship with time is a design principle. If we measure our worth by the approval of others, or by how much we own or what we can do, we are again applying a particular design principle in our life. These design principles shape our world. Our perception of the world right now is the result of the nest of design principles we have fallen into the habit of applying over many years.

Most of us have not deliberately chosen the design principles we apply every day. They are so close and familiar to us that we are wholly unaware of them. Consequently, these unconscious patterns of thought and behaviour are more like default principles than design principles. But whether we apply such principles by default or by design, they carry the same creative potency. They shape our world.

The only way to undo a negative design habit is by developing a positive counter-habit. If we begin applying optimal design principles in our life, we can redesign our world, transforming it into an optimal space. When we consciously choose our design principles, we are engaged in the art of "conscious living" or "living with intent".

≠ LEARNING FROM POOR DESIGN ≠

We are each free to select our own design principles. Some design principles lead to fear and anxiety. They are disempowering and detrimental to life, and create stagnation and suffering. Other design principles are life-enhancing and sustainable. They revitalize our world. They create a space that relaxes, inspires, awakens, comforts and heals. We can know the quality of a design principle by the results it brings.

We will look briefly at a few examples of poor design. These are design principles that work against us, drawing us into dysfunctional ways of living. In India, poor design in life was known as "ignorance" or "foolishness".[36] By understanding folly, or what leads to distress, we can better understand Dharma, or what leads to human flourishing. We will look at six examples of poor design. I have chosen them because they are especially common today.

(1) Losing Ourselves in the Endless Search for Worldly Worth

Mostly, when people speak or do something, they are trying to make a point. If we listen and watch carefully, usually, beneath it all, that point is: "I'm worth something. I'm lovable." Every day, countless people assess their own worth. They work extremely hard to measure up to society's criteria for worth. Very few are immune to this struggle.

We find ways to inflate our sense of worth, but then we experience it depreciating. Our sense of worth inevitably remains fragile and under continual threat. This is because no situation is ever permanent or safe. Achievements are quickly forgotten, and must continually be renewed. Looks fade, businesses and investments fail, and skills decline or become obsolete. Recognition and appreciation are fickle, and easily lost. Thus, our self-esteem is subject to continual weathering and erosion.

As soon as our sense of worth depends on something that is not fully under our control, we will have a great fear of that thing. Our sense of worth is never safe; and so we are troubled by insecurities. When we derive our identity from what is changeable, the result is fear.

Self-esteem is a fairly recent idea that took hold in California in the 1980s. The term was coined by American psychologist William James in 1890.[37] Most people are taught to think of self-esteem as a good thing. Some even believe it is essential for success. But the Rishis of India were able to see the error in deriving our sense of worth from the play of form in this world.[38] If we are trying to enhance our sense of worth, it means that right now we consider ourselves deficient. The pursuit of self-worth is therefore the plugging of an emptiness within, and is evidence of poor design. Far better than self-esteem is unconditional self-acceptance and unconditional other-acceptance.

Today, this is supported by psychologists such as Albert Ellis, who offers perhaps one of the strongest critiques of the concept of self-esteem. Rating and valuing behaviours and characteristics is useful and even necessary; but rating and valuing human beings' total selves, Ellis argues, is irrational, unethical, absolutistic and destructive.[39] Similarly, Roy Baumeister at Florida State University in Tallahassee points to amassing evidence that instead of building up children's egos we should instead be fostering their self-discipline.[40]

Self-esteem is not the same as self-confidence, or a "can-do" attitude, where we believe we are capable of accomplishing something.[41] It is not the same as trusting ourselves. There is a difference between thinking, say, "I am better than most of the other people in this company" and "I can reach my business targets if I apply myself."

Self-confidence is helpful; but the game of self-esteem is in the end harmful. It is when we search for our own worth in the contents of our field of perception. It is like a monarch searching for her sense of worth, for her identity, in her own kingdom. How is it possible to govern well if we are continually seeking ourselves in that which we are supposed to be governing?

Our continual search for worth is one of the biggest obstacles to being able to consciously create our world. It makes us lead a small human life, binding us in fear to the ordinary. On that fateful day when we first started judging our own worth and the worth of others, we brought a curse upon our world – the curse of anxiety.

When trapped in the self-esteem game, we begin to develop the habit of measuring ourselves against others, and we raise our own expectations to higher and higher levels. As soon as we can afford to move to a more expensive neighbourhood, we begin comparing ourselves against our new, more affluent neighbours. We feel inadequate beside them. Now we have to work still harder and take even greater risks, which leads to higher levels of stress. Life becomes an arduous struggle marked by anxiety and perpetual dissatisfaction. Our lives become extremely heavy, weighed down by a compulsion to prove ourselves, and by the ineluctable need to find grounds to love and accept ourselves. The self-esteem game causes us to feel shame, or the feeling we are not enough just as we are. We long for acceptance, approval, appreciation and applause.

In fact, nothing at all is valuable in our world until we make it so. The judgments and beliefs of others have power over us only when we ourselves choose to believe in them, when we ourselves assimilate them into our world. We, the self, are therefore the origin of all worth in our world. We are transcendent to worldly worth. No earthly value can be placed on us.

We often speak about the importance of being "centred" or "grounded". What does this actually mean? It means finding a place beyond the assignment and measurement of worth, beyond the fickleness of human judgments and opinions. To find our centre means to find the sacred self, unburdened and immovable, before it began seeking its own worth in the temporary world of objects and events.

In India, the first duty of a monarch was to find that place of groundedness. Without finding that centre, a ruler was liable to vacillate between triumph and despair, pride and shame. They would employ all the resources of their kingdom simply to preserve and bolster their own petty sense of worth.

To engender self-esteem, some people repeat positive affirmations to themselves. Others visualize themselves surrounded by people who are patting them on the back or shaking their hand, or standing clapping them. All these techniques keep people within the same thinking – the paradigm of self-esteem. Indeed, they simply reinforce that paradigm. Whether someone has high or low self-esteem, they are ultimately trapped in a self-effacing paradigm. This is because they are falsely assigning a material value to the self, the living origin of worth. To step beyond self-esteem is to completely free ourselves from comparison. When we do this, we create a perfect space for our own unique nature and potential to manifest.

(2) Taking Our Story Far Too Seriously

We are each a storyteller. Our story is our life. We can't help but fashion what psychologist Dan McAdams describes as an "evolving story that integrates a reconstructed past, perceived present, and anticipated future into a coherent and vitalizing life myth."[42] We are not only the author of our story, but also the lead character in it. We carry this story with us wherever we go. We can never escape it. Our story is the script from which our life unfolds.

So much of our story is inherited. From a young age, we are told what to be like, how to behave, what to want and hope for, and what to fear. We internalize these ideas unthinkingly and uncritically. We carry them into our story.

We come to believe we are what we wear, what we drive, what we watch and what we watch it on. We work very hard to keep up appearances. We try to live up to so many expectations and pressures. Slowly, imperceptibly, we build the walls of our own confinement.

With everyone living out their personal story, we are in the end simply interacting with each other's projections. We view everyone else through the lens of our own story, and our stories can conflict and collide. If we start altering our story, or if we move out of it, it affects other people's stories too. It creates ripples of disturbance in their world.

The story we create for ourselves is just that: a story. The problem arises when we forget this and begin taking our story with utmost seriousness. We are artists who have become so enamoured by our own creation that we have lost ourselves in our own art. We become so engrossed in our story that we lose sight of our own separate existence outside that story. As a result, we take ourselves far too seriously. Our tiny human lives suddenly take on enormous significance.

It is a strange absurdity of life that we truly believe our own story. When the lead character gets into trouble or fails, we are anxious, stressed and dejected. When the lead character triumphs, we are temporarily jubilant. We have a life-long investment in our story and in the lead figure of that story, with whom we identify. The problem with taking our story so seriously is that it not only delimits the way we see, but governs our every move. By buying into our own narrative so wholeheartedly and unthinkingly, we trade away our inner freedom. The more we believe our story, the more we are its prisoner.

Our narrative can make us do the strangest things. We need only look at the lives of those around us, and all the high drama unfolding there.

Taking our story so seriously, and searching for our identity in it, is an example of poor design. It leads to fear, lamentation and confusion. Fear is misery related to how our story may unfold in the future. Lamentation is misery related to how our story has unfolded already. And confusion is misery related to the way we are being fooled by our own story right now, in the present moment.

We forget that the lead character in our story is fictitious. She is birthed by the mind. The ancient texts of India refer to the fictitious self as *ahankara*, which in Sanskrit literally means "I-making". Mostly we live from this fictional self. We, the powerful storyteller, remain undiscovered.

When we become a victim of our own story, we turn our back on our potential. We become our own worst enemy, what the Rishis called a "killer of the self".[43] We begin to lead small, anxious lives. Trapped in our story, we experience a world of want with few possibilities. Our life is marked by constant struggle and striving. Living can feel more like a burden than a privilege. Thus, we continually look for some form of escape from our life.

Everyone has to have a story, or narrative. This is how we make sense of the world. But when we take this so seriously that we forget it is just a narrative, it leads to limitation and suffering. The illusory spell of the narrative is revealed in our behaviour. It shows itself in the way we live. Whenever we find ourselves overcome by anxiety, anger, jealousy, frustration, resentment, dissatisfaction or despair, it signals that we have lost ourselves in our story – we have been swallowed up by the illusory world of a self-created myth.

In ancient India, the powerful hold that our narrative has on us was known as "illusion". The Sanskrit word for illusion, *maya*, means "not that". As we will see, when we invoke Dharma, we free ourselves from the bondage of this myth. The illusion that our story is real causes us to live in a feverish dream. Dharma is about taking back authorship of this text. Releasing ourselves from our text creates instant inner freedom. Learning to consciously author the text of life and direct the way it unfolds is a tremendous ability sufficient to transform our world.

(3) Blindly Pursuing an Idea of
Success that Is Not Our Own

Our story can make our life painfully oppressive. There is a lot to live up to. Our family and friends, as well as the media and advertising industry, tell us what it means to be "successful". All too often, we find ourselves buying into a dream that is not our own, and that does not accord with who we are. We may allow that idea to direct the entire course of our life.

We each have a unique set of gifts, and a particular contribution to make in the world. Our gift may be an unusual capacity to inspire others, an ability to change the way people think, or the devotion to nurture a student or a child. If we are continually trying to conform to the expectations of others, we never give ourselves the chance to manifest who we are meant to be.

We tend to judge some gifts as somehow superior to others. We are quite right. The best gift of all, at least for us, is the one we ourselves already have. In nature, an oak tree pushes out acorns. It doesn't try to push out lilies. It is perfectly happy being an oak. As an oak, it expresses its own perfection perfectly. It doesn't try to pretend to be anything else. It is complete just as it is. If only we could be like that.

One of the strange things about life is that no matter how hard we try, we remain incomplete and unfulfilled until we are perfectly ourselves. When we express ourselves unreservedly, and are no longer ashamed of who we are, we become beautiful. Not just in our own eyes, but in the eyes of everyone around us. By manifesting our purpose, we add beauty to the universe. When we ignore the seed of potential within us and try to become someone we are not, we feel unfulfilled and frustrated. We may spend years meeting all the criteria for today's idea of "success", but if we are not manifesting our natural gifts we will never be beautiful.

So many of us are eager to awaken the giant within. But what if there is no sleeping giant there: what if there is a perfect rose, a mermaid, or a king. There may not necessarily be a multi-millionaire giant within each of us. There may be something infinitely more fascinating and beautiful, if we can only discover it.

The idea that we need to become something, or fit a particular mould, or else we are a "nobody" is very coercive. The underlying assumption is that all people are inherently worthless, until they somehow rise above others and outdo them. This ideology all too often makes people deny who they are. How much peace we would bring into our world if we could just be, rather than try to be somebody.

Nurses who provide palliative care to dying patients learn a lot about the important things in life. When long-time nurse Bronnie Ware questioned dying patients about any regrets they had or anything they would do differently, the number one response was, "I wish I'd had the courage to live a life true to myself, not the life others expected of me."[44] When faced with our own mortality, what stands out most clearly is always the quality of the choices we made in our life.

(4) Continually Waiting for Our Life to Begin

Many of us believe our happiness lies somewhere out in the future, and not in the present moment. We are in the habit of working *towards* happiness, rather than allowing ourselves the possibility of happiness right now. That way of living shapes our world. It is another prime example of poor design.

We spend most of our life putting off life. We are so busy getting ready to live that we hardly have time left to live. Working tirelessly, we suffer many inconveniences and indignities to pursue a set of dreams, which we imagine will make us happy. These dreams, we quite often believe, lie just around the corner, within fairly easy grasp. But in pursuing the horizon, all we ever find is more horizon.

As a result, our world becomes one of perpetual discontent or dissatisfaction, even amidst great abundance. We are unable to find happiness even in what we have worked so hard to acquire. As *Boston Globe* columnist Ellen Goodman observed:

> Normal is getting dressed in clothes that you buy for work, driving through traffic in a car that you are still paying for, in order to get to the job that you need so you can pay for the clothes, car and the house that you leave empty all day in order to afford to live in it.[45]

If the life worth living exists for us somewhere out in the future, it implies our life right now is not good enough. This way of seeing becomes a habit. In other words, we develop a habit of looking at life as deficient. This, then, is what we are bound to experience in any future that emerges for us in the present. We become habituated to a world characterised by lack, or emptiness. No external circumstances will erase that habit of ours.

Our future will never be any better than how we are accustomed to creating our present. The way we are habituated to perceiving the present right now is the way we will also perceive it in the future. As we will see, when we invoke Dharma in our life, we are fully present to life as it unfolds. We are able to experience the full depth of the present moment.

(5) Living in Constant Opposition to Time

In today's time-driven, clock-obsessed world, we never seem to have enough time. We are concerned about falling "behind time", and are eager to be "on time" or better still, "ahead of time". We speak about "beating time" and "racing against time". In short, we live *against* time. In fact, time seems to have become our worst enemy.

We discussed the case of James Henry Paine, the "millionaire tramp". We may well consider James's peculiar habits a sign of mental disorder, but what James does in relation to money, so many of us do in relation to time. After all, we even say "Time is money".

The United States and United Kingdom are among the poorest nations in the world because their populations are time poor. We have what we might call a time-deficit disorder, or TDD. We have devised ingenious ways to do things more quickly, but we have less time than ever before.

We say time is money, but time is something infinitely more valuable than that. Time is life. To live in constant opposition to time is to live in constant opposition to life. How strange, then, that we should choose to adopt an approach whereby we are not on the same side as life, but are working against it. The opposite of life is death. To work in opposition to life is therefore to adopt a death-orientated approach to living.

Our attitude towards time plays a great part in forming our perceptual world. It is one of the most important features of the underlying architecture of our world. Someone who lives in accord with Dharma enters into vital engagement with life; and in doing so, regards time not as her adversary but as her greatest ally.

(6) Believing We Can Get Away with What No One Sees

Even as far back as five hundred years ago, Niccolò Machiavelli observed astutely that "the great majority of mankind are satisfied with appearances, as though they were realities, and are often more influenced by the things that seem than by those that are."[46] When we discover this about people, we may be tempted to hide behind appearances ourselves. We may also start believing, as many do, that we can get away with things – deceit, betrayal, manipulation, back-biting, hypocrisy – so long as we are not found out.

But actually, we don't get away with anything. We are always affected by what we do. Ends never justify the means;

because the means we use create our perceptual world. They form the architecture of the world we inhabit. The belief that there can be no consequences to what we do is our final example of poor design. By living in accord with Dharma, we begin to see that everything we do has creative potency. We are so used to directing our perception outward that we don't see the hidden architecture we are constructing beneath the play of form in our life.

⚡ THE FIGHT FOR OUR INNER FREEDOM ⚡

Imagine living with all six of these habits for our entire life. When we blindly adopt damaging habits, they restrict inner freedom and control us. We are not aware how much self-limitation we collect in our personalities. These patterns, which ossify over the years, are very difficult to undo. Inner freedom is the ability to see and alter our design habits. This ability brings spaciousness and possibility to our world. It allows us to live in an enlarged world of choice.

Our outer freedom is a gloss that all too often hides an inner life that is unsatisfactory. Amidst all our choices we are imprisoned; amidst our comforts and amenities we remain anxious and dissatisfied.

We can feel our inner "unfreedom". Life has for so many become a dull affair, filled with mental struggle. As D. H. Lawrence put it, "We have buried so much of the delicate magic of life."[47] For some reason, many of us have lost sight of the beauty and vibrancy of living. It is as if we have interred life itself, the most precious thing there is. We have become alienated from the dynamic, vibrant undercurrent of life. Despite our unprecedented outer freedom, most of us feel trapped in a very small life. We long for spaciousness. We long for vitality and renewal.

Because we have a certain degree of choice in our external freedom, and because we are in the habit of directing our attention outward, we falsely believe we are free. This creates a danger. As Goethe famously observed, "None are more hopelessly enslaved as those who falsely believe they are free."[48] There is no better way to suppress our own power and potential than to believe in the limitations we assign them.

Today, inner freedom is more important than ever. This is because there are continuous silent pressures on it from all sides, especially through the relentless assault of the media and advertising. Erich Fromm explains:

> Modern capitalism needs men who co-operate smoothly and in large numbers; who want to consume more and more; and whose tastes are standardised and can be easily influenced and anticipated. It needs men who feel free and independent, not subject to any authority or principle or conscience – yet willing to be commanded, to do what is expected of them, to fit into the social machine without friction; who can be guided without force, led without leaders, prompted without aim...[49]

Similarly, Noam Chomsky warns, in the final words of one of his books:

> For those who stubbornly seek freedom, there can be
> no more urgent task than to come to understand the
> mechanisms and practices of indoctrination. These are easy
> to perceive in the totalitarian societies, much less so in the
> system of "brainwashing under freedom" to which we are
> subjected and which all too often we serve as willing or
> unwitting instruments.[50]

Our inner freedom is under full siege, but we are asleep to this. We are so used to directing our attention outward into the realm of objects and events that we are mostly unaware of the vast inner territory that has already been taken from us. We are so focused on having, that we have lost sight of what it means to be. As a result, we have relinquished the most valuable resource there is: not oil or gold, but our inner freedom, which is the ability to choose our own design principles.

⋟ DESIGNING A FULFILLING LIFE ⋞

A tiger in the wilderness is an elegant, majestic and powerful creature – a breathtaking sight. She commands attention. When this same animal is imprisoned for too long, its wild, free spirit is subjugated. Caged in a zoo, the captive animal begins to develop strange patterns of behaviour. Its eyes become glazed. It paces endlessly up and down. Humans are like this too. In our unfettered and free state, we are beings of immense power. But when we are imprisoned in a death-orientated perceptual world – a world filled with anxiety, unease, dissatisfaction and other toxic forces – we begin to adopt strange patterns of behaviour. We fall into self-destructive habits.

Our physical universe conforms to certain laws – such as the law of gravity and the laws of thermodynamics. But our perceptual world has laws also. We call these laws "habits". Our habits determine what kind of world we inhabit. If we change our habits, we change our world.

By consciously applying design principles in our life, we can create a perceptual world that supports us. Good design principles will be directed not at the play of form in the field of perception, but at the *faculty of perception* itself. They will alter the hidden architecture of our world. They will do this by modifying the inner mechanisms that shape our world, such as our attitudes, desires, direction of attention, beliefs, relationship with time, and sense of identity. They will seek to alter our perceptual world not at the level of effect, but at the level of *origin*.

The quality of the design principles we apply right now determines the quality of our life right now. Good design principles awaken our full potential and bring happiness into our world.

We all seek happiness in life, without exception. Happiness is our primary duty. As Robert Louis Stevenson noted, "There is no duty we so much underrate as the duty of being happy."[51] Of course, by "happiness" I am not referring to some kind of beaming, bovine contentment. I mean the free flourishing of our powers. If we define happiness in this way, as the ancient Greek philosopher Aristotle did, then the aim of the teachings of Dharma is to help us fulfil our most important duty of all, our duty of happiness.

To help us invoke Dharma, the Rishis devised the Dharma Code, a set of principles that operate as universal laws. The Dharma Code has its origins in the Vedas, the oldest texts on earth in continuous use. We will turn to the Dharma Code in the next chapter.

Notes

36. The term used in Sanskrit is *ajnana* or *avidya*. Key verses on the subject of ignorance include *Shri Ishopanishad*, 10; *Bhagavad-gita*, 4.42 and 10.11; and *Bhagavata Purana*, 3.32.38, 4.12.15, 6.17.18, 7.7.27 and 10.4.26

37. Laura Spinney, "All About Me", *New Scientist*, Vol. 214, No. 2862 (28 April 2012), p. 47. See Roy F. Baumeister and John Tierney, *Willpower: Rediscovering Our Greatest Strength* (2012). William James defined self-esteem as the ratio of a person's successes to their "pretensions" or goals. In other words, it is a subjective measure of our own value that increases as we achieve our goals. These days, self-esteem has also acquired the second meaning of "an unduly high opinion of oneself; vanity", leading to an inflated ego.

38. *Ahankara*, or false ego, arises when we identify with the contents of the field of perception. This manifests as our search for our worth in objects and outcomes. The self, however, is separate from the play of form in the field of perception. Whatever is visible in the field of perception is not us. To look for ourselves in the field of perception, in our perceptual universe, is like searching a movie for a view of the cameraman. The texts of India therefore explain that *ahankara* is a product of illusion. For instance, see *Bhagavad-gita*, 3.27 and *Bhagavata Purana*, 3.26.16 and 11.13.29.

39. See Albert Ellis, *Feeling Better, Getting Better, Staying Better* (2001); and Albert Ellis, *The Myth of Self-Esteem* (2006).

40. Laura Spinney, "All About Me", *New Scientist*, Vol. 214, No. 2862 (28 April 2012), p. 47. See Baumeister and Tierney, *Willpower*.

41. Roy F. Baumeister, Jennifer D. Campbell, Joachim I. Krueger and Kathleen D. Vohs, "Exploding the Self-esteem Myth", *Scientific American Mind*, Vol. 16, No. 4 (December 2005), pp. 50–57.

42. Dan P. McAdams, "Can Personality Change? Levels of Stability and Growth in Personality Across the Life Span", in T. F. Heatherton and J. L. Weinberger (eds.), *Can Personality Change?* (1994), p. 306.

43. For example, see *Shri Ishopanishad* (Mantra 3) and *Bhagavata Purana* (11.20.17).

44. Bronnie Ware, *The Top Five Regrets of the Dying* (2011), pp. 34–43.

45. As quoted in John de Graaf, David Wann and Thomas H. Naylor, *Affluenza: The All-Consuming Epidemic* (2001), p. 36.

46. Niccolò Machiavelli, *The Prince and the Discourses* (1940), 1.25.

47. D. H. Lawrence, "Cypresses"; in D. H. Lawrence, *The Complete Poems of D. H. Lawrence* (1994), p. 236.

48. Johann Wolfgang von Goethe, *Goethe's Opinions on the World, Mankind, Literature, Science, and Art* (1853), p. 3.

49. Erich Fromm, *The Art of Loving* (1995), p. 67.

50. Noam Chomsky, *Knowledge of Language: Its Nature, Origin, and Use* (1986), p. 286.

51. Robert Louis Stevenson, *Essays of Robert Louis Stevenson* (2008), p. 40.

CHAPTER 4

THE DHARMA CODE

"WHERE THERE IS DHARMA,
THERE IS VICTORY."

– Mahabharata[52]

L IFE IS MORE than the duration between birth and death. It also has a hidden dimension – Dharma. By our actions and thoughts, we move up or down on this vertical dimension. It would not be incorrect to call the dimension of Dharma the *dimension of divinity.* Dharma elevates or ennobles us. It lifts us from the level of the ordinary and manifests the god-like within us. We are impoverished as human beings when we focus on the horizontal dimension of duration and lose sight of the vertical dimension of Dharma.

Heaven and hell are both contained within us, and we know this from experience. The teachings of Dharma are intended to situate us in the heavenly part of ourselves. This then allows us to use the quality of that realm to shape our life. If we can discover that realm within, we have invoked the higher self. Because this is where the higher self resides, in the abode of the gods.

Dharma exalts us. It is the unfolding of excellence – when everything we think, say or do creates optimal outcomes.

Dharma is excellence in the beginning, in the middle and in the end. Excellence in the beginning is *optimal thinking*. Excellence in the middle is *optimal choices*. Excellence in the end is *optimal outcomes*. When we follow the path of Dharma, our fate tends towards optimal outcomes.

Dharma allows us to inhabit life more fully. A person who is aware of the hidden dimension of Dharma understands only too well that it's possible to pass an entire lifetime never truly having started living. As Oscar Wilde observed, "To live is the rarest thing in the world. Most people exist, that is all."[53]

When we think about our life, we tend to focus on our age (our position in the dimension of duration). But this way of looking at life is not very helpful, because we have no control over our age. When we focus instead on the dimension of Dharma in the present moment, we become far less concerned about the past or the future. Age does not trouble us. If anything, it brings greater practice and experience in living in accord with Dharma. This approach is empowering. After all, the extent to which we apply Dharma in our life is something we can choose at all times.

To help us navigate the hidden dimension of Dharma, we turn now to the Dharma Code, an ancient method for invoking Dharma in our everyday life. The Dharma Code is concealed in Sanskrit texts, whose deeper meaning has been passed down in several different lineages of masters, called *sampradayas*. Never before has the Dharma Code been openly disclosed in such detail outside one of these lineages.

⚡ CAN LANGUAGE HELP US UNCOVER THE DHARMA CODE? ⚡

One important feature of Dharma is that it is impartial. Not only does Dharma operate in the same way for everyone, it also doesn't favour one area of our life over another. It functions at such a deep level in the architecture of perception that it revitalizes all areas of our life. When we manifest Dharma, we express our best in all the domains of human experience.

From the dawn of civilization, humans have endeavoured to put their experiences into words; and words have in turn also shaped their way of understanding the world. If we study any language, we immediately find four primary domains of human experience – being, differentiating, relating and doing. I noticed, for instance, that the eight parts of speech in language capture these four domains quite neatly.[54]

The Four Primary Domains of Language

PARTS OF SPEECH	DOMAINS OF EXPERIENCE
1. Nouns 2. Pronouns	Being
3. Adjectives 4. Adverbs	Differentiating
5. Prepositions 6. Conjunctions	Relating
7. Verbs 8. Interjections	Doing

Every language has its own structure; but they all seem to have a way to express these four domains.

We can consider what the highest expression in each of these four domains of human experience might be:

• **Being**. Excellence in relation to what is, surely, is to see things clearly for what they are, and not to close ourselves off to the truth. It is also to live in accord with the way things are.

• **Differentiating**. Our thoughts, words and actions spring from our state of being. The highest expression in the domain of differentiating is therefore the ability to distinguish between what uplifts us and what degrades us, what nurtures and what pollutes us. It is the ability to recognize what promotes the conditions of human flourishing and also what destroys those conditions, both for ourselves and for others.

• **Relating**. What better form of relating is there than with respect and with love? This begins with doing no harm, and culminates in doing most good.[55] Respect and love are directly opposed to any form of violence. Non-violence is therefore the gateway to being able to respect and love others, as well as ourselves.

• **Doing**. Excellence in the domain of doing is surely about using our full energies to be the very best we can be. As all great sportsmen and women will affirm, manifesting excellence requires the fire of discipline.

⚹ THE FOUR DIMENSIONS OF DHARMA ⚹

Having looked for clues in language, let us turn our attention to the sacred Sanskrit texts on the subject, composed millennia ago. Sure enough, we find in the *Bhagavata Purana* that Dharma has four interlocking dimensions – (1) Truth, (2) Purity, (3) Non-violence and (4) Discipline.[56]

Whenever its four dimensions converge, Dharma flourishes. In other words, one could say Dharma is the meeting point of Truth, Purity, Non-violence and Discipline. The Dharma Code, expressed in its simplest form, is therefore a matrix of these four interlocking principles.

The Dharma Code[57]

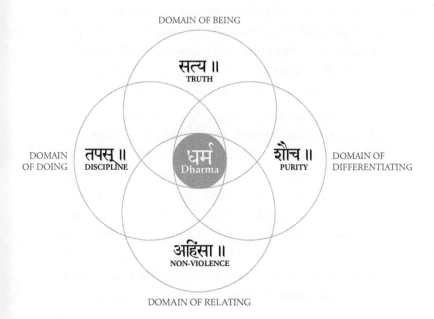

DOMAIN OF BEING

सत्य ॥
TRUTH

DOMAIN OF DOING

तपस् ॥
DISCIPLINE

धर्म
Dharma

शौच ॥
PURITY

DOMAIN OF DIFFERENTIATING

अहिंसा ॥
NON-VIOLENCE

DOMAIN OF RELATING

This means, of course, that each of these four principles needs to be understood and interpreted in relation to the others. Thus, Discipline here refers to focused effort that is also non-violent and grounded in Truth.[58] Likewise, Truth is not a serene state of mind: it must be lived. This entails great Discipline.

The reason we don't manage to invoke Dharma fully is that we don't usually apply all four Dharma principles together. We usually apply just one of them, or at best two. This is like pushing down on the acceleration pedal of a car while simultaneously leaving three handbrakes partially on.

When we want to achieve something, the Dharma principle we tend to reach for immediately is Discipline. In other words, we want to put in as much effort as possible. But if our effort is in the wrong direction, how can it yield an optimal result? Discipline in the Dharma Code is therefore not effort, but "right effort". The secret to invoking Dharma in our life is therefore not to apply one of the Dharma principles, but to apply all of them, simultaneously.

It's important to understand how the four dimensions of Dharma work together. For example, if we oppose the Dharma principle of Non-violence by exploiting and harming others, we pull ourselves into illusion. In other words, we oppose Truth also. For instance, when the Germans persecuted the Jews in the 1930s and 1940s, they first had to invent the lie of Jewish inferiority. They began to think of Jews as something less than human, portraying them in anti-Semitic literature and Nazi propaganda picture storybooks for young children as rapacious liars and thieves, vermin-like, grotesque and immoral, the Devil in human form, and an ever-present danger to the well-being of German society.[59] The German people would not have been capable of hurting the Jews without first creating, and believing, these lies about them.

Likewise, when we choose to ignore Truth, we inflict a form of violence upon ourselves and upon others. A similar dynamic exists also between Purity and Discipline. For example, Purity, or discerning what helps us from what harms us, is futile if it is not brought into action through Discipline. Thus, each of the four Dharma principles relies upon the other three to flourish.

Uncovering our full potential is an integrated endeavour. It requires practice in and a deep understanding of all four Dharma principles. This is because the domains of human experience do not exist in isolation from each other; they are entirely interconnected and interdependent. A failure in one of the Dharma principles will affect our ability to live all of them.

These four Dharma design principles, when applied in our life, actually begin to alter the way we perceive the world. They reshape the architecture of perception. They are therefore principles of transformation. Because they operate in all of the domains of human experience, the four dimensions of Dharma lead not to partial transformation, but total transformation.

⸙ UNCOVERING OUR FULL POTENTIAL ⸙

We are each like a crystal or precious gem. When placed in the light, we exude our inner lustre, our natural magnificence; and when kept in darkness, we conceal our splendour. We long for the light of life to shine from within us in all its luminosity and reveal our brightest colours. To reveal our hidden luminosity is to invoke Dharma in our life.

Dharma is "right action", which uplifts us and leads to optimal outcomes. But "Dharma" also has a second, closely related meaning – that of "true nature", or the "law of a thing's being".[60] The Dharma of an acorn is to become an oak. The Dharma of a river is to flow to the sea. Our Dharma is to manifest our potential, by freeing ourselves from habits of inferiority to our full self.

Within an acorn, invisible to our human eye, is a sturdy three-hundred-year-old oak. That tree exists in the acorn in the form of compressed potential. Until an acorn grows to become a mighty and venerable oak, its Dharma remains an unexpressed potential. We too carry an invisible potential within our being. Each of us has a unique set of gifts, a concealed magnificence. We awaken that potential when we apply the Dharma Code in our everyday life.

If the gemstone of the self remains in obscurity for many years, we may lose sight of our purpose. As the years drift by quietly and we age, we settle for a banal and ordinary life. We lose faith in who we are, in our luminosity; we forget the extraordinary potential that lies asleep within us. We come to believe a lie: the lie of our own ordinariness.

This lie is birthed from darkness. It leads us to abandon our purpose, to relinquish our destiny. This is the moment something within us fades. We begin to die on the day we stop searching for the best in ourselves.

⚡ WHAT IS IT WE WERE PLACED ON EARTH TO DO? ⚡

The Dharma of a knife is to cut well; the Dharma of an eye is to see well. What exactly is our Dharma, then? The Dharma Code, when applied in our life, will begin manifesting an answer to that question for us naturally. Trying to define our purpose now, when we may have little idea of what we are capable of, would simply be artificial. Any such definition would simply be an expression of our own present limitations. After all, there may be many facets to us that we are not fully aware of just now. Our full potential will reveal itself to us naturally in due course as we apply the Dharma Code in our life.

Young graduates are regularly encouraged to "find their passion" and then to "pursue their dreams". This advice, which is regularly dished out at graduation ceremonies, is actually misguided. Most successful young people don't look inside and then plan a life. They don't take an inward journey and come out having discovered a developed self, ready to meet the challenges of the world. No, *living* allows them to find themselves. By confronting challenges in life, by finding a problem that summons their energies, they discover what they are capable of and what is important to them. In other words, our potential or purpose manifests not through a process of cogitation, but through our vital engagement with the world.

Not just any kind of engagement will do, of course. To manifest our potential, we need vital engagement – the kind of engagement that summons all our energies and draws out the best in us. To that end, the Rishis of India devised the Dharma Code. One could say the Rishis were sages of potentiality. They were experts in what lies hidden to the human eye.

⸎ LIVING IN ACCORD WITH DHARMA ⸎

If we look back at the times we accomplished extraordinary things, we will see it was through the perfect execution of these four Dharma principles. Likewise, if we look back at moments of great embarrassment in our life, we will be able to trace them to a failure to live by one or more of these four principles. Truth, Purity, Non-violence and Discipline are the lodestars of Dharma, guiding us to human excellence. These principles are therefore potent "change agents" in life.

An example of the Dharma Code in action in the twentieth century is the life of Mahatma Gandhi – which served to inspire other leaders like Martin Luther King Jr and Nelson Mandela. Gandhi was a frail old man with few possessions. But he tried to cling tenaciously to Truth, Purity, Non-violence and Discipline. Gandhi called his movement *satyagraha*, or "Truth Force".[61] He strongly advocated Non-violence. So potent were these forces that they eventually defeated the British Empire, the largest and mightiest colonial empire that ever was, which at its height occupied nearly a quarter of the world's land area. Without lifting a sword or firing a single shot, Gandhi eventually forced the British Empire to relinquish its "crown jewel", India.

By invoking Dharma, a humble human being can become known by millions of people as Mahatma, a "Great Soul". This is what Dharma does: it uplifts. When someone who practises Dharma speaks, people cannot help but listen. The words of such a person connect deeply; they cannot be ignored – because they are the voice of Truth. In trying to live the Dharma Code, Gandhi invoked something much larger than he was. He awakened an ancient sleeping power, a universal potency.

In ancient Indian culture, the primeval power that sustains is traditionally worshipped as Vishnu, the All-pervading One. Thus, when philosopher-kings lived out the ancient Dharma Code, they sought to invoke the universal potency of Vishnu.

While the Dharma Code generates potency and strength, it will not erase tragic circumstances in our life. It can, however, make it a little easier to face them. It gives us resilience in the face of adversity. It grants us the courage and intelligence to deal even with extremely difficult situations in the best way possible.

Yudhisthira, an emperor in the royal Kuru Dynasty of India, was unfairly cheated of his entire kingdom in a rigged game of dice and exiled to the jungle with his wife and brothers. He endured intolerable hardship for thirteen years. But he never relinquished Dharma.[62] We too may go through periods of personal hardship in our life, but if we live in accord with Dharma, we retain our inner sovereignty. In the end, like Yudhisthira and all those who embody Dharma, we will emerge victorious.

⚹ TRANSGRESSING DHARMA ⚹

Most of us already manifest Dharma in our life, at least to some extent. Without any Truth, we would fall into total delusion and dementia. Without any Purity, we would be without a redeeming virtue, and would be dragged down by destructive forces like anger, self-loathing, resentment and guilt. We would become alcoholics and drug addicts. Without any Non-violence we would become brutes, and would probably find ourselves incarcerated or killed before long. Without any Discipline at all, we would fall into degenerative indolence and self-loathing.

We see this only too clearly in historical rulers who totally disregarded the principles of Dharma – King Zhou of Shang, Herod, Caligula, Nero and Hitler. They lived in direct opposition to Truth, Purity, Non-violence and Discipline. Hitler was not only violent and untruthful, but also highly undisciplined, falling into bouts of depression punctuated by fits of rage. Sometimes, military leaders do display Discipline; but that quality manifests Dharma only if it is refracted in the other three Dharma principles. Only then is it "right action", or behaviour that leads to optimal, vital and sustainable results.

All habits of foolishness, grand or petty, degrade us (literally: bring us *down*). They do so because they pull us down on the vertical dimensions of life, Dharma. For instance, when we believe our story so much that we forget it is just a story, we live in opposition to Truth. When we measure our own worth and the worth of others, we not only oppose Truth but also inflict a form of violence on ourselves and on others.

By applying the Dharma Code, we adopt a new approach to life. This manifests in our life as innumerable new counter-habits – habits of Dharma. We begin creating new laws in our perceptual world. In other words, we begin to construct our world out of Truth, Purity, Non-violence and Discipline.

⚹ HOW TO INTERPRET THE FOUR DHARMA PRINCIPLES ⚹

How is the Dharma Code to be applied? How should these four principles be interpreted? To gain a deeper understanding, I began scrutinizing the Medieval Sanskrit commentaries on the subject, approaching elders in my tradition to deepen my understanding, and systematically applying the Dharma Code in my personal life.

The purpose of the Dharma Code is to help us overcome habits of foolishness, by creating habits of excellence. The Rishis sometimes refer to this endeavour as yoga, or "skill in action".[63] Most people think yoga is a series of body postures and breathing exercises. But this is only a small part of yoga, to aid deeper introspection.[64] Traditionally, before even attempting postures and breathing, the student of yoga would cultivate habits of excellence, among which these four principles of Dharma feature most prominently.[65]

Now we may think that "Truth", "Purity", "Non-violence" and "Discipline" are simple enough to grasp. But actually they each embody a universe of meaning, which reveals itself naturally to us through self-awareness and thoughtful application. Expressed in what is an abbreviated form, the four Dharma principles are simply aids to memory, or prompts – akin to what is referred to in India as a *sutra* (literally: a "thread").[66] If we have a spool of thread and can locate the tip of the thread, we can quickly unravel the entire spool – which may extend for hundreds of yards. Thus, each of the four Dharma principles is the tip of a thread, and contains a spool of meaning. In the next four chapters we will unravel some of this meaning.

Notes

52. For example, *Mahabharata*, 6.21.11, 6.41.55 and 6.62.34.

53. Oscar Wilde, *Soul of Man under Socialism* (1891); published in Oscar Wilde, *Collected Works of Oscar Wilde* (1997), p. 1046.

54. Grammar books occasionally classify words into ten parts of speech, by including *numerals* (i.e. numbers) and *articles* ("a" and "the"). In many cases, however, these can be treated as adjectives, and for simplicity I have therefore chosen to ignore them. In basic terms, nouns and pronouns denote people, places and things. They express what is. Adjectives and adverbs serve to qualify, helping us make differentiations. Prepositions and conjunctions establish relationships between things. Verbs are *doing* words. Interjections, or expressions of emotion, also convey a kind of doing – one that occurs within us.

55. Thanks to Michael Geary of Cranmore Foundation for this observation.

56. The four dimensions of Dharma are *satya* (Truth), *shaucha* (Purity), *ahimsa* (Non-violence) and *tapas* or *tapasya* (Discipline). *Ahimsa* is occasionally substituted with *daya* (compassion) or *anrishamsya* (non-cruelty). In the *Bhagavata Purana*, these four Dharma principles are said to be the legs of Dharma, who assumes the form of a white bull (1.17.24). These Sanskrit terms are referred to also in the Vedas and Upanishads. *Satya*, for instance, is referred to in the *Chandogya Upanishad* (3.17.4), *Brihad-aranyaka Upanishad* (1.3.28) and *Mundaka Upanishad* (3.1.6). *Ahimsa* appears in the *Taittiriya Samhita* (5.2.8.7) of the *Yajur Veda*, the *Kapisthala Katha Samhita* (31.11) of the *Yajur Veda*, and several times in the *Shatapatha Brahmana*. It also appears in the *Chandogya Upanishad* (3.17.4 and 8.15.1), which prohibits violence against all creatures. The earliest reference of the word *tapasya* is to be found in the *Rig Veda* (7.82.7a), which also has dozens of references to words derived from *tapas*. The word *tapas* is mentioned also throughout the Upanishads, including the ancient *Chandogya Upanishad* (3.17.4).

57. Illustration by Michael Geary. Used and adapted with permission.

58. For example, the *Bhagavad-gita* defines *tapas*, or Discipline, in three verses: 17.14 (*tapas* of the body), 17.15 (*tapas* of speech) and 17.16 (*tapas* of the mind). Interestingly, *tapas* of the body includes *ahimsa* (Non-violence) and *shaucha* (Purity), and *tapas* of speech includes *satya* (Truth). This illustrates the interconnectedness of the four Dharma principles. See also *Bhagavata Purana* (5.5.1), which states that Discipline creates Purity, which in turn leads to true and lasting happiness.

59. For instance, see Elvira Bauer, *Trau keinem Fuchs auf grüner Heid und keinem Jud auf seinem Eid* [trans. *Trust No Fox on his Green Heath and No Jew on his Oath*] (1936). See also Mary Mills, "Propaganda and Children during the Hitler Years" (The Nizkor Project).

60. The translation of Dharma as "true nature", "defining property", "essential attribute" or the "law of its being" follows a long commentarial tradition, and can be related to Rig Vedic usages where *dhárman* can mean "foundational nature". See, for instance, Alf Hiltebeitel, *Dharma: Its Early History in Law, Religion, and Narrative* (2011), p. 97. See also Shrila Bhaktivinoda Thakura, *Jaiva-dharma* (2008), Ch. 1.

61. *Agraha* means "insistence", and therefore also has the sense of "force".

62. The life story of Yudhisthira and his brothers, known collectively as the Pandavas, is told in India's great Sanskrit epic the *Mahabharata*.

63. *Bhagavad-gita*, 2.50. The *Bhagavad-gita*, traditionally regarded as a treatise on yoga, defines yoga as "skill in action" (*yogah karmasu kaushalam*).

64. In traditional *ashtanga-yoga*, postures (*asanas*) and controlled breathing (*pranayama*) are the third and fourth stages of an eight-stage yoga process.

65. In his *Yoga Sutras*, Patanjali lists Non-violence (*ahimsa*) and Truth (*satya*) as the first two *yamas*, or habits of restraint in the practice of yoga; and he lists Purity (*shaucha*) and Discipline (*tapas*) as the first and third *niyamas*, or habits of cultivation in the practice of yoga.

66. A *sutra* is an aphorism, or a concise statement of principle or precept. Such statements are often so terse as to render them virtually incomprehensible without the help of a qualified teacher within a legitimate discipular line.

II

THE FOUR DHARMA PRINCIPLES

CHAPTER 5

TRUTH

THE SOUND OF BRASS BELLS echoed from temples in the distance. It was 4:30am and I was on the flat rooftop of the monastery. The dark shape of the Yamuna river was visible under the full moon, as it wound its way slowly to the distant sea. A million stars sparkled in the sky like silver dust cast into the heavens. Among them, the full moon shone with striking brilliance. A solitary conch shell resounded nearby.

I descended for the early morning ceremony in the monastery, and then returned to the rooftop to continue my morning meditation. Gradually, dawn emerged. The sun, a magnificent globe of fiery red, began to pierce the veil of mist that covered the horizon. I always marvelled at how quickly the sun rises in India. If you keep your eye on it, you can actually watch its ascent, like a sacred goblet of fire being passed from the Earth to the Sky, to illuminate the world.

As a monk, we pray each morning in the language of the ancients for the light of wisdom to dispel the darkness of ignorance in our heart. As part of my practice, I had made a vow not to shave or wear shoes for four months. Today was the final day of this vow. If you had asked me what day of the week or month it was, I wouldn't have been able to tell you. I had almost entirely lost track of the Western calendar, and now kept count of the days by the phases of the moon. Today was the full moon day at the end of the sacred month of Karttika in 1994. It was the day my teacher would initiate me into the *sampradaya*, the lineage of masters and students in which Dharma teachings have been passed down for generations.

One of the monks shaved my head and thick beard with an Indian razor. After bathing in the cold morning water, I applied *tilaka*, a sacred marking, in golden clay to my forehead. Each *sampradaya* has its own distinctive mark. Ours is a long U-shape with an inverted leaf-like design below it. It represents the footprint of divinity – an emblem of Vishnu, the Guardian of Dharma.[67]

I applied this same mark to twelve places on my body in the way my teacher had taught me, while reciting mantras, or sacred Sanskrit syllables, for invoking the presence of Vishnu. This constellation of resplendent marks creates an armour to protect one from the forces of illusion that cover or obscure Truth. Since Vishnu manifests as the Dharma Code, I was in a sense wearing the Code on my person.[68] I could feel its intense protective potency. It renders a mortal body made of bones, tissue and blood into a temple of Vishnu, a sanctuary of Dharma.

Clean shaven and dressed in the garb of a monk, I now approached my teacher. Born in 1921 in Bihar, India,

Shrila B. V. Narayan Goswami had joined the monastic order in 1946. "Narayan" is a name of Vishnu that means "the resting place of all beings".[69] My teacher had studied the ancient Dharma texts from childhood in the venerable Bhakti tradition and embodied these teachings throughout his life. Here, I knew, was a veritable Rishi – a teacher of the highest order who had a profound understanding of the ancient lore, not just in theory but in practice.

My teacher explained that spiritual life begins with Truth. This means, first of all, understanding that human life is meant for cultivating wisdom. A genuine student is not satisfied with the superficial, but strives to develop a deeper vision that allows him or her to look beyond life's illusions and see the true nature of things.

"How does a student master Truth?" I asked.

My teacher looked at me with his piercing blue eyes. "Do not try to be a master of anything. Try to become a servant of Truth.

"A practitioner is dedicated always to the highest Truth," my teacher continued, "and this is reflected in his thoughts, words and actions." He then wrapped a string of small beads made of sacred Tulasi wood around my neck in three rounds.

"This represents complete dedication by body, mind and words," he explained. In that act, I was accepted into the ancient lineage of Vishnu.

⊰ TRUTH IN OUR THOUGHTS, WORDS AND ACTIONS ⊱

What did it mean to be a servant of Truth? Over the next few months, my teacher taught me many things, including the qualities of a true teacher and the importance of guarding against hypocrisy.

"Many people are eager to instruct others," he said, "but to find someone who actually practises what they teach is exceptionally rare."

To help me understand, my teacher told a story of a boy in Mathura who was addicted to eating sweets. Every day he would consume large quantities of delectable confections such as *laddu* and *jalebi*, finding all manner of creative ways to procure them. The boy gradually gained a lot of weight. He also began suffering from boils. His mother tried to get her son to stop eating so many sweets, but without success. She explained that sugar damages teeth, triggers weight gain, feeds cancer cells, and promotes premature ageing; but nothing could alter the boy's habit. She therefore asked the family guru to speak to the boy.

"I would like to help," the family priest said, "but I'm sorry, I cannot speak to the boy right now. Give me a month. I will then be able to help him."

The mother agreed. One month later, the family priest returned. He had a short talk with the boy, and the boy did not eat another *laddu* or *jalebi* again. The mother was delighted, and bewildered in equal measure.

"What did you say to my son?" she finally asked. "And why did you insist on waiting a full month before speaking to him?"

"You see, since childhood I have been addicted to sweets myself," the priest confessed. "If I had told your son a month ago to give up sweets, I would have simply been a hypocrite. Also, my words would have carried no potency. To help your son, I first needed to help myself. I needed some time to understand how to give up sweets. Having learned an effective way to overcome my own habit, I was able to help your son overcome his."

My teacher's words affected me deeply. I began thinking of all the ways that my actions don't match my words, and my words don't match my thoughts. Then, in the course of my study, I came across the following Dharma dictum in a collection of teachings for princes, which seemed to confirm what my teacher had been explaining:

> The low-minded person thinks in one way, speaks in another, and acts still differently; but the great soul, or Mahatma, says what he thinks, and does what he says.[70]

I pledged to try to become simple-hearted and live more like a Mahatma. This, I understood, was the first step to a life of Truth. We encounter so many people who ignore this basic principle: smokers who tell their children not to smoke, Marxists who wear Calvin Klein, people at conferences discussing social inequality and injustice as they sip expensive champagne and eat strawberries, people who say they love animals but also eat them, people who speak ill about their colleagues and friends behind their back.

Life is full of these contradictions, and we just get used

to them. Eventually, we become so used to adapting and conforming to meet expectations that we become entrenched in our own lies. We forget who we are and what really matters in our life.

In Oxford and Cambridge I met many intelligent and privileged individuals who seemed lost and alienated from themselves. We can become so busy "presenting" ourselves that we don't know anymore who we really are. Later, when we try to rediscover Truth, it can be very difficult – because we have spun such an extensive web of untruth in our life.

The Rishis predicted that in Kali-yuga, the present age of machines and quarrel, "hypocrisy will be accepted as virtue."[71] The personification of this age is sometimes depicted as an impostor king who is smashing the legs of Dharma, who has taken the form of a white bull. Dharma's four legs are its four principles, beginning with Truth.[72] In other words, a lack of Truth is now the normal state of affairs. To live a life of Truth is largely to flow against the current of today's world – no easy task.

⚜ WHY TRUTH IN OUR THOUGHTS IS POTENT ⚜

The voice of the mind is continually feeding us statements, which it dresses up as "truths":

> "*This person is really quite irritating.*"
> "*She is embarrassing me.*"
> "*She has to sort out her life.*"

We usually believe such statements of the mind unquestioningly, and act on them. We allow them to upset us and make us resentful and angry.

But if we stop and think about it, how many of the things we tell ourselves are actually true? Mostly, they are simply inventions in our own small story, which we project on to others. No one "has to" do anything. No one but we ourselves is the cause of any of our own emotions.

Many people also tell themselves they can't do something, or most damaging of all, that in some way they are not enough just as they are. When we make these judgments and believe them unquestioningly, we veer away from a simple life of Truth. This inevitably draws suffering into our life.

We oppose Truth with our thoughts whenever we refuse to see things clearly about ourselves, about others, or about our situation. People eating a hamburger tell themselves the cow they are ingesting probably led a happy life and didn't suffer much when it died. We prefer to believe that our fashionable clothes or shoes weren't produced by exploited factory workers or child labour abroad. Generally speaking, in life we are engaged in a long compromise with Truth. Not to be so engaged is exceptionally rare.

Truth in our thoughts is about not telling lies to ourselves. If we lie to ourselves, we will necessarily repeat those lies when we speak to others; and all the while, we will believe we are telling the truth. Thus, we cannot be honest with others if we are not first honest with ourselves, if our life is itself an expression of lies.

We are actually creatures of Truth. We recognize Truth when we encounter it, just as we know when we are awake that we are awake. The more we live in accord with Truth, the more easily we also recognize untruth when we come upon it.

Why is Truth so potent? Because Truth does not need to be sustained in any way: it sustains itself. Thus, if we can build our life on Truth, the life we build will be upheld by the universe itself. It requires no additional effort on our part.

We can kick Truth about as much as we like and it won't bend out of shape. Winston Churchill put it well: "[The] truth is incontrovertible. Panic may resent it, ignorance may deride it, malice may distort it, but there it is."[73] The lies we tell ourselves, by contrast, are brittle and fragile. They are vulnerable to being shattered at any time. Maintaining them requires a lot of hard work. No matter how much we try to fix or plaster over the cracks of falsehood, new cracks always keep emerging somewhere.

Allegiance to Truth leads to perfection in the domain of existence, the field of what is. The I Ching affirms this same wisdom: "It is only when we have the courage to face things exactly as they are, without any sort of self-deception or illusion, that a light will develop out of events, by which the path to success may be recognized."[74]

⚡ WHY TRUTH IN SPEECH IS POTENT ⚡

Once, a senior monk sent me to the rooftop to pick leaves from the sacred Tulasi plant for a ceremony that was about to take place. A few minutes later I returned with a small handful of leaves and presented them to him. The ritual was about to begin. Almost a hundred pilgrims and guests were present.

The senior monk turned to me and asked if I had washed the Tulasi leaves. I hadn't. But to my surprise, I found myself saying that I had. I was horrified at myself. The monk, who had himself adopted a vow of Truth, could detect the untruth instantly. "Go wash them a second time," he said kindly.

I felt terrible the whole day. I had lied, and to a senior monk. That evening, the monk, without saying anything further about the incident, told us the following story from the Vedas, the oldest texts of India.

Gautama Rishi, the son of Haridruman, was renowned for his wisdom and mastery of sacred lore. A young boy named Satyakama longed to study under the Rishi. One day, he told his mother, Javala, about his wish. Javala agreed readily, although Satyakama was still only a child. She was very happy that her son was interested in training for the highest knowledge.

Gautama Rishi taught many students at his forest hermitage. To be admitted into his pupillage, a prospective student needed to present his father's family name, because in those times teachers accepted students only from certain families.

"Dear Mother, of what family am I?" Satyakama asked, knowing full well that Gautama would want to know his family lineage.

This presented a problem. Javala had never been married, and Satyakama was an illegitimate child. He would therefore probably be denied the right to study the Vedas. Javala was embarrassed to have to explain this to her son. She thought to herself, "If I tell my son the truth, he will be shocked to hear that his parents weren't married when he was born. And if and when he explains this to Gautama Rishi, the sage may be scandalized, as will the other students listening. News will get around, and whoever hears our story will judge us harshly and treat us unkindly."

Javala wavered for a while, but then she resolved to be honest with Satyakama. She would bequeath her son the truth. Javala kissed her son gently on the head, and said to him, "My dear boy, when I was a girl, I lived in poverty and served many men in different countries as a slave girl. Your mother has never been married. I am Javala. So tell the sage that your name is Javala Satyakama."

Later that day, Satyakama made his way to Gautama Rishi's hermitage, on the edge of the forest. The boy bowed to the teacher with respect. "Revered Sir, will you accept me as your student?" he asked. "With your blessings, I wish to become a knower of the sacred lore."

"My dear boy, what is your lineage?" Gautama asked kindly.

Without fear, Satyakama told the sage what his mother

had disclosed to him. He then traced his descent from his mother, saying, "Javala is my mother; I am Satyakama; so I would be known as Javala Satyakama."

It was a startling disclosure. Gautama looked at the boy, an embodiment of Truth. The sage rose from his seat and embraced him warmly. He said, "My child, bring wood for the sacred fire. I have decided to accept you as my pupil. You have not swerved from the truth. Only one from the best of families can utter such truthful words without hesitation or compromise."

In the course of time, under the guidance of his teacher, Satyakama attained enlightenment. Incidentally, Javala had selected a fitting name for her son. Satyakama means "Seeker of Truth". Those committed to the Dharma principle of Truth are able to understand all the confidential teachings of the Rishis – not only intellectually, but as living wisdom.[75]

When we maintain Truth in our speech, both to others and to ourselves, our speech becomes imbued with great potency. Truth has a power, the senior monk explained. The Rishis therefore advise us to be impeccable with our speech and never to turn it against ourselves.[76]

As children, we usually said things just as we saw them, without compromise. A child's simple observations are unaffected and unbribable. In the words of Emerson, they sink "like darts into the ear of men, and put them in fear."[77] But as we grew up, we began increasingly neglecting Truth and uttering lies. Our words stopped matching our thoughts.

Why are truthful words so potent? Because when we speak

Truth, the universe speaks through us. As Mahatma Gandhi observed, "I may be a despicable person, but when Truth speaks through me I am invincible."[78]

⚡ WHY TRUTH IN BEHAVIOUR IS POTENT ⚡

The first company I worked for upon graduating from university was a dot-com. I was a copywriter. This was back in 1999, at the height of the dot-com bubble. As a start-up, the company had many ideas and lots of energy to make them happen. But like many other Internet companies at the time, we had no clear path to revenue – even as we ramped up our annual spend to over £500,000. The business quickly burned through its venture capital, and despite the best intentions and efforts, nothing could save it from eventual collapse.

This was my first learning experience in business – and for me a crash course in the Dharma principle of Truth. We can ignore reality, but we can never ignore the consequences of ignoring reality. Despite outstanding creative talent and successful PR, we had inadvertently ignored the unforgiving basic realities of business. The start-up therefore failed.

We can learn a lot about Truth by looking at the ways we choose to avoid or ignore it. When my younger brother David was undergoing intensive chemotherapy in a fight for his life, there was something I saw at the St Bartholomew's Hospital in London that shocked me. Whenever I walked in through a particular side entrance, I encountered one or two patients with lung cancer, looking pale and deathly from their chemotherapy, silently puffing away at cigarettes in the bitter cold. It was a startling sight.

We each have our own ways of ignoring Truth. Only when we act in alignment with Truth, or the reality of things, are our efforts self-sustaining. The Dharma principle of Truth is about seeing things clearly. When refracted through the principle of Discipline, it also implies living in accordance with what we know. In other words, it implies living with integrity and impeccability.

Unfortunately, we are often deluded by the fog of untruth. This may take outward form as denial, blaming, resistance or excuses. In my own life, I have fallen "out of Truth" several times, and while I have learned from these experiences, they always led me into a hard but futile struggle and to inevitable defeat.

In the end, I learned, our failure to acknowledge Truth, or what is, always leads to defeat. This is why the Vedic texts declare, "Truth alone triumphs; not falsehood."[79]

⚚ BEING TRUE TO OUR OWN NATURE ⚚

A cow is able to transform grass into milk; a hummingbird can stop mid-flight and hover in the air; and a fish can draw oxygen out of water. Every animal has a particular gift, or "power". We too each have our own unique nature and capabilities. We are not all built the same way. To recognize this and be true to our nature is also part of what it means to live in alignment with Truth through our behaviour.

Unfortunately, we have learned to live with many masks. As La Rochefoucauld observed, "We are so accustomed to disguise ourselves from other people, that in the end we disguise ourselves from ourselves."[80] Gradually, we have lost interest in the right to be authentic, a right we exercised naturally as children. We find ourselves saying what we think others want us to say, even if we don't mean it, and doing what others expect us to do, even if we know it isn't right for us.

Truth is about insisting always upon ourselves and never pretending to be anybody else. It is about relinquishing façades and disguises. When we dishonour who we are, we live against Truth. This brings instability and weakness into our life.

Truth always begins at home, with oneself. As Shakespeare advised so directly, "This above all: to thine own self be true".[81] He was emphasizing the first dimension of Dharma. When we live in accord with Truth, our own North Star, our life is not a hard struggle to be somebody. No. Just as a tree doesn't strain to grow, and just as a river doesn't struggle to flow to the sea, we manifest our purpose naturally, through "effortless effort".

Notes

67. Vishnu as the Guardian of Dharma: see, for example, *Bhagavata Purana*, 1.12.11 and 11.4.5, as well as *Bhagavad-gita*, 4.7–8 and 11.18. The *tilaka* mark also has deeper and more esoteric meanings.

68. *Bhagavata Purana*, 11.17.11. Vishnu manifests as the white bull of Dharma, whose four legs are the four Dharma principles. The *Bhagavata Purana* states that by applying Dharma principles, a person pleases Vishnu (*Bhagavata Purana*, 7.11.8–12; see also *Shri Narada-bhakti-sutra*, 78). The Bhakti tradition teaches that the pinnacle of Dharma is to take complete refuge of Vishnu, the upholder of Dharma (e.g. *Bhagavad-gita*, 18.66; and *Bhagavata Purana*, 1.2.6 and 6.3.21).

69. *Ayana* means "resting place", "refuge" or "abode", and *naras* means "of living beings".

70. *Hitopadesha*, 1.102. The *Hitopadesha* ("Good Instructions") is a collection of teachings for young princes composed by Vishnu Sharma on the request of King Dhavalachandra. Many of its verses can be traced to the Dharma teachings found in the Puranas and Itihasas.

71. *Bhagavata Purana*, 12.2.5. The *Bhagavata Purana* states also that hyprocrisy is the offspring of *adharma*, the absence of Dharma (4.8.2); and the children of hypocrisy are greed and cunning (4.8.3).

72. *Bhagavata Purana*, Canto 1, Ch. 17.

73. Winston Churchill, speech in the House of Commons, 17 May 1916.

74. Hellmut Wilhelm and C. F. Baynes, *The I Ching or Book of Changes* (1967), p. 25.

75. This story originates from the *Chandogya Upanishad*, 4.4.1–5. In the thirteenth century, Marco Polo was surprised by the integrity of the brahmins of India. "No consideration whatever can induce them to speak an untruth, even though their lives should depend upon it," he reported. (Marco Polo, *The Travels of Marco Polo, a Venetian, in the Thirteenth Century* [1818], p. 662.)

76. For instance, see *Bhagavata Purana*, 8.22.29–30, 11.11.29 and 11.18.16. See also *Brihad-aranyaka Upanishad*, 1.3.28.

77. Ralph Waldo Emerson, "Self-Reliance", from *Essays: First Series* (1841).

78. Mahatma Gandhi, *The Epic Fast* (1932); in *Gandhi: All Men Are Brothers* (2004), p. 67.

79. *Mundaka Upanishad*, 3.1.6. (M. A. Mehendale argues for an alternate translation in "*Satyam eva jayate nanritam*," *Journal of the American Oriental Society*, Vol. 81 [1961], pp. 405–8.)

80. La Rochefoucauld, *Collected Maxims and Other Reflections* (2008), p. 35.

81. William Shakespeare, *Hamlet*, Act 1, Scene 3.

"WE ARE WHAT WE THINK.
ALL THAT WE ARE ARISES WITH OUR THOUGHTS.
WITH OUR THOUGHTS WE MAKE THE WORLD.
SPEAK OR ACT WITH AN IMPURE MIND
AND TROUBLE WILL FOLLOW YOU
AS THE WHEEL FOLLOWS THE OX
THAT DRAWS THE CART.

"WE ARE WHAT WE THINK.
ALL THAT WE ARE ARISES WITH OUR THOUGHTS.
WITH OUR THOUGHTS WE MAKE THE WORLD.
SPEAK OR ACT WITH A PURE MIND
AND HAPPINESS WILL FOLLOW YOU
AS YOUR SHADOW, UNSHAKABLE."

– Buddha[82]

CHAPTER 6

PURITY

W E TURNED THE CORNER, and there she was: the sacred Ganges, revered across India for her purifying influence. As we approached the riverbank, several black-faced Hanuman monkeys, almost as tall as humans, filed past us. They made their way on two legs towards an old man, who was distributing peanuts.

Across from us, the Ganges was joined by the dark waters of the Jalangi, and for many miles the two rivers, one dark and one light, flowed side by side without merging together. Large Ganges river dolphins sported along the divide. With their square pectoral fins and very long beaks, they resembled strange aquatics from another age. These magical sightless creatures would suddenly leap out of the water, delighting the children and pilgrims being ferried on wooden boats across the breadth of the river.

This was the ancient small town of Navadwip, brimming with life and activity. At the time of the Sena Kings, it was the capital of Bengal and a great seat of learning. Young students would travel from across India to study Sanskrit, philosophy and Vedic lore here. The region had once been filled with lakes, orchards and forests screaming with colourful orchids and dazzling flowers. Wild elephants once pushed their way through the heavy jungle, while deer darted through the undergrowth. Royal Bengal tigers prowled through the tall grasses at the edge of small villages.

We paid our homage to Ganga-devi, the goddess of the river. A damsel of incomparable beauty, she is depicted as having a lustre like the bright champak flower. She rides on a *makara*, a sea dragon with a mouth of a crocodile, a body of a fish, and a tail of a peacock. In India, the Ganges is believed to have immense purifying properties, having been consecrated by the touch of Vishnu. We offered burning incense sticks to the goddess, sticking them upright into the clay riverbank. We also offered jasmine flowers and lustrous red rose petals, which drifted into the distance on the river's powerful current. We then bathed in the sacred river.

The ancient texts list Purity as one of the "divine" attributes, a quality of great sages and Dharma rulers.[83] I knew there was a lot more to Purity than merely bathing in the morning. I asked the elderly monk I was with, whom we addressed affectionately as Pujari Prabhu, to tell me what he had learned and understood about Purity.

"Purity means to make our heart a sacred space, so that Vishnu may reside there," the monk began. His golden skin gleamed in the sunlight. "The sacred texts predict that in Kali-yuga, the present age, people will consider themselves clean and ready to face the world if they have simply taken a bath.[84] We may clean our body and wear perfumes and creams, but what about the state of our mind and heart? Do we ever pay much attention to that?"

⚹ SURDAS AND THE SEWAGE CLEANER ⚹

To help me understand, the monk told me about an intelligent student named Surdas, who burned with eagerness to learn the deeper meaning of the Vedas. He had a wise guru, whom he approached for instruction. But his guru directed him to practise Purity in his life for one month and then return to see him.

Exactly one month later, Surdas bathed and put on fresh, clean clothes. Eagerly he made his way to his guru's home for advanced lessons. On the way, a street sweeper, who was going about his work carelessly, accidentally brushed dirt on to Surdas's clothes.

"What are you doing, you idiot!" Surdas shouted angrily. "Now I'm impure, and have to go back, wash and change. What a waste of my precious time."

Unknown to Surdas, his guru saw everything that had just occurred. When Surdas returned a short while later, his guru said, "Dear Surdas, you are not yet ready for further lessons. Come back in another month."

Surdas accepted his guru's wish and returned home. When another month had passed, Surdas bathed and put on his best clothes, which gleamed in the sunlight. As he made his way through an alley, the same sweeper, who happened to be there, brushed his dirty broom against Surdas, leaving a foul-smelling streak of black filth across Surdas's side.

"You stupid idiot!" Surdas exclaimed, stuttering with rage. "You did that on purpose, didn't you? You imbecile. If I weren't on my way to see my guru right now, I would teach you a fine lesson you would never forget."

Like the last time, Surdas's guru sent the student away for another month. When that month came to an end, Surdas again made his way to his guru. This time the sweeper spotted Surdas from a distance. He remembered how Surdas had berated him for what had merely been an accident. Indignant, the sweeper this time deliberately hurled the contents of his waste container on to Surdas. Sewage and filth spattered over the student and dripped from his clothes.

But this time the sweeper was taken aback. Surdas folded his hands with respect and said kindly, "Dear sweeper, I thank you. You are my teacher, for you have taught me how to overcome my anger."

As Surdas approached his guru's home, he found his guru waiting for him. "Surdas, you have mastered the principle of Purity in your life," his guru said. "You are now eligible to understand the deeper meanings of the sacred texts."[85]

"You see, there is more to Purity than simply taking a bath in the morning," Pujari Prabhu chuckled, as he looked into my eyes. I realized in that exchange that if I can make my very being a sacred space from which to act, then whatever I do throughout my day will be highly potent and beneficial.

There are qualities that nurture life, like gratitude, humility and light-heartedness. There are also qualities that inhibit life, like anger, resentment and discontent. Purity is about differentiating between what sustains life and what inhibits life. It's about *choosing* what we allow into our perceptual world. We need to protect our world from noxious forces that would distort and contaminate it. Purity is the ability to keep our life clean and unpolluted.

The Rishis of ancient India advise us to have a heart as pure as crystal. The purer a crystal is, the more transparent it is. Purity brings clarity to our life, and deep insight. It allows us to think, speak and act from a position of wisdom.

As humans, we tend to accumulate a lot of baggage. That baggage clouds our judgment and weighs us down. We accumulate that excess baggage in our mind. Purity is about letting go of the unwanted. It's about removing that which is unhelpful. We know we are living in accord with Purity when we feel clear, inspired and alive.

⸕ WHATEVER WE FEED GROWS ⸕

One evening, a wise village elder told his grandson about a fierce battle that occurs within our world. "The battle is between two 'wolves' within each of us," he said. "These wolves are fighting for supremacy over our world. One wolf is evil: it is anger, hate, fear, shame, arrogance, self-pity, guilt, greed, contempt, resentment and inferiority. The other wolf is good: it is love, gratitude, harmony, truthfulness, beauty, humility, kindness, hope, compassion, courage and generosity."

The little boy thought about it for a minute and then asked his grandfather, "Which wolf wins?"

The old man replied simply, "The one you feed."[86]

Whatever we dwell on in our life, we feed; and whatever we feed, grows. Therefore, it's best to dwell only on what we want to fill our universe. Most of us wouldn't intentionally ingest anything toxic. We are fairly careful with what we eat. But we regularly and knowingly allow noxious emotions and attitudes to enter and pollute our world. We do this largely by dwelling on them. We also do it by keeping the company of people whose perceptual worlds are filled with toxicity.

Our attention plays a key role in shaping our reality. Whatever the mind dwells on increases in significance. It fills our world. When the mind focuses on something, it magnifies it. Conversely, whatever the mind lets go of diminishes in significance. This is easy to understand. If, for instance, we close our eyes and focus all our attention on listening, we begin to hear sounds that were until then lost to us – the rustle of the trees, the soulful chirping of birds, the laughter of children.

Attention is our mind's zoom tool. It enlarges everything in its field. If we dwell on our fears, we enlarge them. If we dwell on people's faults, all we begin to see are faults. In the Bhakti tradition, it is said that when we focus on the faults of others, we build a bridge by which these faults enter our world. If, however, we take the time to reflect upon and appreciate the good qualities of others, we invite those qualities into our life. What we focus on, we become.

Negative energies like anger, frustration, lamentation and anxiety cannot tolerate positive, vibrant, life-sustaining energies. There is nothing they look upon with more hostility. This is because such positive energies are wholly incompatible with them; they spell the death of these negative forces. What follows is a struggle for survival – a battle between darkness and light within the depths of our being. The energies we focus on most are the energies that thrive and survive. Our attention is the food that allows them to grow in strength.

People sometimes wonder why the things they fear, so often occur. They wonder why what they resist persists. Most people are thinking about what they don't want. They then wonder why what they don't want keeps showing up in their life again and again. It can feel almost as if the universe is responding to our thoughts. This is because the universe we experience is in fact largely created through perception. Whatever we focus our attention on we magnify.

⚡ PROTECTING OUR WORLD ⚡

The enlightened person, the texts of India say, is like a swan.[87] According to popular lore in India, if you give milk mixed with water to a swan, the majestic bird is able to extract the milk and leave aside the water. The idea is that an enlightened person has the ability to nurture her world with the good by dispossessing it of the unwanted. The idea is simple enough; but its actual practice is one of life's most difficult arts.

Psychologists speak about life stories that can show a "contamination" sequence.[88] This is when the story we like to tell is about positive events being compromised by misfortunes. We begin constructing limiting and debilitating interpretations that take our narrative down unhelpful, and even harmful, pathways. People who create these kind of stories are, unsurprisingly, more likely to suffer from depression.[89]

When we are overcome by negativity, often we don't even notice it. It clouds our perception, compromising our ability to make powerful choices. When our environment is healthy and vital again, we may look back with surprise, and even disbelief, at how we have behaved.

To protect our world, it's important to make the "field of now" a sacred space, free from negativity. If someone always carefully protects this space – the field of now – she protects the full extent of her perceptual universe. This is because all of life unfolds in one place only: the here and now. This is the arena of life, the sacred enclosure that needs protection.

⚡ THREE STAGES OF CONSCIOUS CREATION ⚡

In guarding against negativity, there are three stages, or levels of ability:

Stage One. At first, we are able to recognize a negative or disabling force, and its harmful effect, but only after that force has already passed through our world and wreaked its havoc. Of course, we can understand these forces in a theoretical way before they arrive. But the moment they actually enter our world, their turbulence alters our state of being. Our power to discriminate is impaired, and we lose perspective and do things we may later come to regret deeply. Only afterwards are we able to reflect on what occurred and understand that our world was hit by a destructive storm.

Stage Two. With some practice, we can recognize negativity as it actually enters our world. Our very awareness in the present moment actually provides a measure of release, and we find we are able to avoid making important decisions or taking action in that compromised place. We see the negativity clearly, even if we cannot fully avoid or extinguish it. What we are able to do is recognize and tolerate it, by sitting it out. There are many things in life that are outside our control. They often enter our world, and we are not strong enough to keep them out. But eventually they pass, as surely as they arrived, like the coming and going of winter and summer.[90]

The key to mastering the second stage is to become more attentive to our feelings, which are signals. Our thoughts can deceive us, but our emotions never lie. They always speak the truth. If our emotions are negative, then it means our thinking is negative also. Negative emotions are therefore a wake-up call. They signal that our world is under siege. One who is astute is able to spot these signals early on.

Stage Three. Still more difficult is to be able to recognize a negative or disabling force, like anger or fear, as it emerges in our world, and then also to hold it off or even to transform it into a positive force. This is possible by taking shelter of positive forces, such as hope, gratitude, love and compassion.

Some people are able to enter a room of edgy or depressed people and immediately shift its energy, without even uttering a word. They can summon immense powers of creativity, so that even the uncreative feel creative around them. They can make the uneasy feel easy and the fearful feel safe. They can give hope to the hopeless and courage to the weak. With their words, they can bend the consensual reality of a group towards a better path.

Negative emotions are the sworn enemies of positive emotions. The two cannot sit alongside each other in the assembly house of the heart. They immediately fight each other for dominance. By nurturing one, we are able to conquer over the other. The texts of India sometimes refer to this struggle as the eternal battle between gods and demons that takes place in the depths of all humans.[91] By nurturing the god-like qualities within us, we overcome our lower natures.

⋆ NURTURING OUR WORLD ⋆

When we see something, it doesn't just walk in through our eyes. We have to fire our attention at it, like an arrow. As the philosopher Edmund Husserl recognized, consciousness is *intentional*.[92] For example, if we look at our watch absentmindedly, without this act of "intentionality", we don't see the time, and have to look again.

We are continually firing our attention at things; and through this intentional act, we shape our world. We have the ability to alter our world by altering the quality and direction of our attention. What we fire our attention at, we invite into our world. What occupies our attention, occupies our world.

Some people try very hard to empty their world of negativity. But emptiness is an artificial state. It's impossible for us, while we are alive, to have no thoughts or emotions at all. Therefore, the way to free ourselves from negative thoughts and emotions is to replace them with positive ones.

My teacher explained one day that if we want to fill a jug with water, it would be extremely difficult to try to empty it of air first. But by filling it with water, we automatically expel all the air. In the same way, the best way to protect our world is to fill it with the positive, flowing currents of life. If we fill our world with love and kindness, we leave no room for hatred and unkindness. If we fill our world with gratitude, we leave no room for want.

I realized this one day as I thought about everything in my life I was deeply thankful for. Gratitude creates immediate abundance. It generates immense positive energy. Studies have shown that talking and writing about what we are thankful for amplifies happiness.[93] If we focus every day on the things in our life we are truly grateful for, we will find that what we are grateful for will keep increasing in our life. Thankfulness is one of the most potent forces for annihilating negative thoughts in our world.

Thoughts are like seeds. If we plant an apple seed into the earth, it would be absurd to expect an avocado tree to grow from that seed. Similarly, we cannot expect happiness or abundance from the thought seeds of dissatisfaction and anxiety.

It's actually better not to focus our attention on negative forces at all – not even to try to fight them off. Our nature is to reflect what we look at. As Friedrich Nietzsche put it, "Battle not with monsters, lest ye become a monster, and if you gaze into the abyss, the abyss gazes also into you."[94] What we look at inevitably enters our world.

In the monastery, we meditate and recite auspicious mantras early each morning, before beginning our day. Why do we do this? We do it to transform our mind and heart into a temple of Vishnu, an abode of Dharma. It ensures we do not begin the day in a dirty place.

⚍ AS WITHIN, SO WITHOUT: AS WITHOUT, SO WITHIN ⚍

The mystics of India explain that the self is like a clear quartz crystal or a diamond.[95] A crystal will reflect the colour of whatever we place it against. If we put it against a red cloth, it will shine red; if we place it on a blue cloth, it will shine blue. Similarly, our consciousness absorbs the qualities of its environment. This not only includes the company we keep, but also our physical surroundings (e.g. our neighbourhood, workplace), the time of day, our own thoughts and actions, and even the food we eat.[96]

This in itself is almost a truism. If we work or live with negative or fearful people, we will notice how their pessimism or fear tends to rub off on us. But if we surround ourselves with positive, happy people, we tend towards a more optimistic outlook (all other things being equal). If we work in a high-stress, anxiety-ridden workplace, our own stress levels will inevitably rise. If we eat wholesome and fresh food, we tend to feel light and well; but if we eat plenty of junk food, we tend to feel a bit like a refuse bin, at least after a while. As the reputed French gastronome Brillat-Savarin put it, "Tell me what you eat and I will tell you what you are."[97]

Even the presence of a dog has been shown to affect people's attitude. According to recent research by Christopher Honts at Central Michigan University, a playful dog can shift people's attitude and help them collaborate more effectively. Those who had had a dog to slobber and pounce on them ranked their team-mates more highly on measures of trust, team cohesion and intimacy than those who had not.[98] This principle of "association" applies to all things – people, work, food, pets, neighbourhood, etc.

There is a continual interplay between us and the world: we shape the world and the world shapes us. Protecting our perceptual universe is about choosing what we let into our world. It's about choosing the quality and nature of our experience. This is without doubt one of the most powerful design principles for conscious creation. In setting out the Dharma Code, the *Bhagavata Purana* specifically states that Purity is compromised by harmful association.[99] The implication is that Purity can also be enhanced, through helpful association.

⚘ CHOOSING THE COMPANY WE KEEP ⚘

My teacher showed me by his example what Purity means. Whenever I was in his presence, all sorrow and suffering would immediately withdraw, like the dark night vanishing at dawn. He had this effect on everyone.

In December 2010 my teacher left this world in Jagannatha Puri, India, aged 89. I was with him during his final months, tending to him during the day and night with a few dedicated monks. We would take shifts sitting at his bedside. During the night when it was not my shift, I would sleep very lightly on the floor next to my teacher's bed, and get up quickly if he needed anything.

As my wife will attest, whenever I am in pain or discomfort, I become irritable and unkind. My teacher, however, did not take any morphine or other allopathic painkillers; and yet he showed only the greatest kindness and affection to everyone. He was tolerant, humble and fearless. He always smelled naturally fragrant. I knew I was witnessing the departure of a great devotee of Vishnu, a Rishi who had fully mastered the mind and senses. Fixed in the highest state of yoga, known as *samadhi*, he left this world free from fear, lamentation and confusion.

According to the Rishis, the single best way to manifest our higher nature is by keeping the company of those who are wise or enlightened.[100] This doesn't necessarily mean people who know a lot. It means those who embody Truth, Purity, Non-violence and Discipline in the way they live.

In particular, keeping company means relating with

intimacy.[101] This opens the crystal of our heart to the influence of others. We then imbibe their moods and desires. If we open our heart to people who are judgmental and who are trapped in the cycle of self-seeking, we can become like them. We too will start looking for our own worth in objects and outcomes, and become fearful, beleaguered human beings trapped in a story of our own making.

How is it that the company we keep should be so important? Erich Fromm explains what he refers to as a "law in human relations":

> There is no contact between human beings that does not affect both of them. No meeting between two people, no conversation between them, except perhaps the most casual one, leaves either one of them unchanged – even though the change may be so minimal as to be unrecognizable except by its cumulative effect when such meetings are frequent.[102]

Most parents warn their children against keeping bad company; but not so many parents actively encourage their children to seek out good company. And if they do, their idea of good company is people who come from wealthy, powerful or prestigious families. We tend not to look further than what might promote our material interests. We don't realize that we become like those we habitually spend time with, by imbibing their attitudes and desires.

We may well retain a different intellectual opinion to the people we associate with, and our tastes may differ somewhat too. But the state of our heart will increasingly begin to coincide. If we keep the company of takers, we will reinforce the taker in us; if we keep the company of givers, we will become a more giving person ourselves. This is the alchemical effect of association.

We can feel what degrades us. Likewise, we can feel what uplifts or ennobles us. The sensitivity to make that distinction and the ability to act on it is what the Rishis called "Purity".

Notes

82. Thomas Byrom, *Dhammapada: The Sayings of the Buddha* (1993), pp. 1–2.

83. For instance, see *Bhagavad-gita*, 16.3.

84. *Bhagavata Purana*, 12.2.5.

85. This story was told to me by my teacher, Shrila B. V. Narayan Goswami, in June 2001 and is recorded in my handwritten notes.

86. There are different versions of this folk story, which is commonly but incorrectly attributed to the Cherokee. The story itself is inconsistent with Native American story forms, which do not typically contain a moral at the end. For a detailed discussion about the possible origin of this story, see Chelsea Vowel, "Check the Tag on that 'Indian' Story" [blog post], 21 February 2011.

87. The ancient texts of India often refer to those who are enlightened as *paramahamsa* (literally, "ultimate swan"), or perfected swan-like beings. For example, see *Bhagavata Purana*, 1.18.22, 2.7.10, 6.3.28 and 12.13.18.

88. Jonathan Haidt, *The Happiness Hypothesis: Putting Ancient Wisdom and Philosophy to the Test of Modern Science* (2006), p. 144.

89. M. Adler, E. Kissel, and D. P. McAdams, "Emerging From the CAVE: Attributional Style and the Narrative Study of Identity in Midlife Adults", *Cognitive Therapy and Research* (in press); as quoted in Jonathan Haidt, *The Happiness Hypothesis*, p. 144.

90. See *Bhagavad-gita*, 2.14.

91. See *Bhagavad-gita*, Chapter 16. The traditional Hindu festival of Rama-navami, which celebrates the victory of Shri Rama over the demon Ravana, is popularly interpreted also as representing the triumph of Dharma over the forces that oppose Dharma, in a battle that occurs within each of us.

92. For instance, see Joseph J. Kockelmans, *Edmund Husserl's Phenomenology* (1994), p. 92.

93. For example, M. E. P. Seligman, et al., "Positive Psychology Progress: Empirical Validation of Interventions", *American Psychologist*, 60 (2005), pp. 410–421.

94. Friedrich Nietzsche, *Beyond Good and Evil* (1989), aphorism 146.

95. For instance, see *Hari-bhakti-sudhodaya* (8.51), quoted by Shri Rupa Goswami in *Shri Bhakti-rasamrita-sindhu* (1.2.229): "Like a jewel, a person takes on the qualities of those with whom he comes in contact."

96. See *Bhagavata Purana*, 11.13.4.

97. "Dis-moi ce que tu manges, je te dirai ce que tu es." Jean Anthelme Brillat-Savarin, *Physiologie du Goût* (1848), Aphorisme IV.

98. "Manager's Best Friend: Dogs Improve Office Productivity", The Economist [website] (12 August 2010).

99. *Bhagavata Purana*, 1.17.24. The Sanskrit word *sanga* in the verse means "association", but refers here to unhelpful or harmful association.

100. For example, see *Bhagavata Purana*, 1.18.13 and 10.84.11. See also *Bhagavata Purana*, 11.26.26, as well as *Hitopadesha*, 1.41 and 1.192.

101. For the six types of intimate exchange, see Shri Rupa Goswami, *Shri Upadeshamrita*, 4.

102. Erich Fromm, *The Art of Being* (1992), p. 23.

CHAPTER 7

NON-VIOLENCE

"BEARS, UNLIKE HUMANS, have a baculum," he explained with delight. He waved the pale, thin shaft of bone, which was maybe 15cm long.

The young chap I was speaking to had come from Eton. His father had given him £1 million for his sixteenth birthday. He had used the money to hire a helicopter and fly out to Russia with a few friends from Eton to track down and shoot a bear. While the helicopter hovered nearby to ensure his protection, he had shot a young bear with an automatic weapon. As a trophy, he had severed the animal's baculum, or penis bone, which he now kept in his Cambridge dorm as a cocktail stick.

The year before, he and his friends had gone to Spain and gunned down four hundred geese. He boasted about it, without the slightest sign of remorse. If someone was capable of this kind of violence as a youth merely to amuse himself, I thought, what might he be capable of in a position of power and influence? What would he *not* do to further or safeguard his interests?

I remember my first day as an undergraduate in Cambridge. Proud parents were cheerfully helping their teenage prodigy unload the car, carrying lamps, toasters and newly purchased kitchen ware to college dorms. I had arrived alone by coach, with just a single suitcase and a cardboard box. This more or less represented everything I owned.

At that time, my family lived in Beaumont Leys, one of the worst neighbourhoods in Leicester. Making ends meet had always been difficult. As we grew up, we would never buy Twix bars, Walkers crisps or soft drinks at the corner shop like the other kids. We couldn't afford it. We were happy if there was some food in the house when we returned home after school.

No one in my family had been to university. Guided by the principles of Dharma, I had applied myself diligently and made my way to Cambridge, defying all the odds. Now that I was here, it was with some disbelief that I stepped into this strange new world of the privileged and elite. Doors began to open for me. Clyde & Co., a top City law firm, offered me a training contract. A glittering career in London lay ahead of me, if I wanted it.

But I was uneasy. I had witnessed poverty and inequality first hand: old men dying in the streets of Calcutta, dishevelled children in rags living from street scraps, beggars without any arms who tapped your car window with their head and opened their mouth to accept your change. I felt there was something distinctly wrong about a society in which a few lived with so much privilege, extravagance and waste while the majority elsewhere in the world struggled simply to stave off hunger.

I couldn't help but think that we were living very small, selfish lives. I was at one of the best universities in the world, but I couldn't see much further than my own career progress and salary. And while I might be against hunting and I might never have intentionally eaten meat in my life, I too was caught up in innumerable unseen patterns of violence.

Our aggression need not be physical or obvious. Today, it mostly takes the form of a blind disregard, a closing of our eyes to what is too terrible or inconvenient to recognize. Thus, the cruelty of our factory farms and slaughterhouses is hidden from view. The workers who create our clothes or produce our fruit sometimes live on less than a dollar a day or suffer from pesticide poisoning, but somewhere far away in China, Brazil or Costa Rica. The heaps of garbage we throw out each week are buried or shipped to Africa. Out of sight is out of mind. The Great Pacific Garbage Patch – a swirling mass of floating plastic flecks, bottle caps, toothbrushes, Styrofoam cups and plastic bags – is now the size of Texas, but it is allowed to grow precisely because it lies out of view and doesn't touch our shores.

This was all very disturbing for me. My growing dissatisfaction with the society in which we live made it increasingly difficult for me to participate in it whole-heartedly. I felt lost. At this time, I kept having a recurring dream that my teacher was calling me. I would wake up in the middle of the night at about 3:00am, gripped with intense feelings, tears streaming from my eyes. I took this as a sign. It was time to rediscover my purpose in life, as a pilgrim on a search for wisdom. In the end, I decided against a highly paid career in the City. Instead, I returned to India to try to learn more about the ancient principle of *ahimsa*, or Non-violence.

⚘ REDUCING OUR FOOTPRINT OF VIOLENCE ⚘

"No power on earth can subjugate you when you are armed with the sword of *ahimsa*," Mahatma Gandhi explained.[103] The Rishis had understood that Non-violence is a force infinitely more potent than any form of aggression or coercion. But what exactly is Non-violence and how do we practise it?

The word *ahimsa* means to do no harm.[104] We may inflict harm upon others, upon the environment, or upon ourselves. Sometimes we are not even aware of the damage we cause; at other times, we may simply prefer not to pay attention. *Ahimsa* is about reducing our footprint of violence and exploitation, as far as possible. It is the primary Dharma principle. As the *Mahabharata*, a key Dharma text, affirms, "Non-violence is the highest Dharma."[105]

Interestingly, we find this primary dimension of Dharma in every major culture and tradition. Buddhist teachings, for instance, tell us, "Hurt not others in ways that you yourself would find hurtful."[106] The Jewish tradition teaches, "That which is hateful to you, do not do to your fellow;

this, in a few words, is the entire Torah; all the rest is but an elaboration of this one, central point."[107]   The Bible states, "Do to others as you would have them do to you."[108] Likewise, Islam teaches, "No one of you is a believer until he desires for his brother that which he desires for himself."[109] Confucius gave the same instruction to his students:

> Zigong asked: "Is there any single word that could guide one's entire life?" The master said: "Should it not be reciprocity? What you do not wish for yourself, do not do to others."[110]

Likewise, the Dharma texts of India proclaim, "This is the sum of Dharma: Do naught to others which would cause you pain if done to you."[111] That all these traditions should express precisely the same teaching, almost verbatim, is striking.

⸲ THE GATEWAY TO LOVING OTHERS ⸲

Non-violence, or *ahimsa*, is the restraint of any negative impulse that could harm another. But there is far more to it than this. The principle is ultimately about developing our faculty of empathy and love. Mahatma Gandhi therefore explained, "True *ahimsa* should mean a complete freedom from ill will and anger and hate and an overflowing love for all."[112] This is supported by leading authorities on yoga.[113] Love for all beings begins with Non-violence; and Non-violence is perfected by awakening the capacity to love.

Non-violence is the doorway to loving. Until we master Non-violence, love and affection remain simply empty words.

This is because love and violence are always opposed to each other. If our professed love for someone is violent, it is not love at all. In our society, the word "love" has been devalued. Like all else, love has been turned into a commodity for our own enjoyment. What many of us call "love" is simply what satisfies our ego and gratifies our senses. If someone stops satisfying us, our "love" fades and dies, despite all the ardent professions of love we made only a few months earlier. So as not to misdirect us towards clichéd, self-indulgent love, the third dimension of Dharma is framed as Non-violence, love's precondition.

When we reduce our footprint of violence, the heart is no longer hard and indifferent, but tender and caring. This is its optimal state. When we give up our habits of violence, then compassion and love, which is our natural state of being, can emerge.[114]

⸝ AVOIDING VIOLENCE TO OTHERS ⸝

I noticed that my teacher was always kind to everyone. He was careful never to hurt any creature, not even mosquitoes or poisonous snakes. He never thought of his disciples as his inferiors; rather he saw himself as a servant.

One way we inflict violence on others is through our judgments. My teacher therefore advised me: "Never criticize anyone, no matter what he is doing, not even in your thoughts. If you do, the qualities you focus on will come into you." We go around seeking and measuring each other's faults. We define others by their flaws. My teacher was not like this: he defined us by the highest potential of our soul. I therefore felt he was one of the only people in my life who truly saw me. Most of us don't see others truly; they see only a secondary character in their own small story.

The word "respect" comes from the Latin *respicere*, "to look back at", "to gaze at". This suggests that when we respect someone, we are actually able to see the other person before us. This requires that we abandon all our judgments. As Rumi put it, "Out beyond ideas of wrongdoing and rightdoing, there is a field. I'll meet you there."[115] The field Rumi is speaking about is a space entirely free of all judgment. It is a field of complete Non-violence.

We have grown accustomed to measuring everything about us in terms of personal advantage, profit and loss. Everything becomes an object of exchange and consumption. As renowned social psychologist Erich Fromm observed, this extends even to our relationships of love, where people tend to search out the most attractive "package" of qualities on the personality market, given their own possibilities for exchange.[116]

When we measure the worth of others by judging them, we reduce other human beings – and also ourselves – to the level of commodities. The habit of judging, therefore, is not life-affirming, but life-negating. Whenever we judge others, by ranking them against ourselves on a scale, we efface ourselves in the process too.

All qualities and attributes exist in pairs: stingy and generous, dull and interesting, stupid and clever, irritating and agreeable. One depends upon the other for its meaning. When we think or speak harshly of someone, we implicitly assign ourselves the positive opposite. For example, if I tell my friends that such-and-such person is "positively dull", I am implying that I am at least moderately interesting. I wouldn't seriously condemn someone as a "loser" if I didn't think I was at least on my way to being a "winner". Thus, in thinking or speaking harshly of others, we reinforce our own illusions. We create a false identity for ourselves, which we must then safeguard and protect in our small human story.

We truly see the person standing before us when we see them through eyes free of violence. We are then able to respect people unconditionally, at what we might call the level of the "sacred self", whatever their outward circumstances – whether they are rich or poor, learned or illiterate, spiteful or kind, talented or inept.

⋆ AVOIDING VIOLENCE TO THE EARTH ⋆

Human beings are presently causing the greatest mass extinction of species since the extinction of the dinosaurs 65 million years ago. Our planet is running out of room and resources. Its biodiversity is in peril: if present trends continue, one half of all species of life on earth will be extinct in less than a hundred years. Almost a quarter of the world's mammals face extinction within thirty years, according to a United Nations report, including gorillas, chimpanzees, orang-utans, koalas, kangaroos, rhinos, hippos, cheetahs, tigers, lions, many species of sharks and dolphins, and polar bears.[117] According to one ten-year study, 90 per cent of all large fishes have disappeared from the world's oceans in the past half century, the devastating result of industrial fishing.[118] Scientists are divided over the specific numbers, but many believe the rate of biodiversity loss is greater now than at any time in history.

We have reached a tipping point. Our collective violence is rapidly disfiguring planet earth, the oasis of life that gave us birth. The earth is scarred by decades of deforestation, pollution and global warming.

This tragedy reflects the state of our own collective perceptual worlds, over many generations. In other words, the powerful forces that have disfigured our planet are exactly the same forces that govern our own perceptual world right now. By engaging in violence, we make violence a design principle in our life. The result: a hardening of the heart, a lack of compassion for the suffering of others, an inability to love beyond our own narcissistic self-interest.

At this time, nothing is therefore more urgently called for than a genuine understanding of the principle of Non-violence.

⚄ AVOIDING VIOLENCE TO ONESELF ⚄

It's easy to notice violence from an external source. It's much more difficult to perceive the internal habits of violence we inflict upon ourselves. We are violent to ourselves every time we think negative thoughts, speak negative words, or otherwise act against ourselves. Thus, the principle of Non-violence begins at home, with ourselves.

There is only one way to overcome a harmful habit: to

create a counter-habit.[119] Therefore, giving up habits of violence requires, ultimately, that we develop the counter-habit of compassion and love.

We are each an artist, or author. The best story we can possibly write is one we write with love. This is the most beautiful work of art we are capable of creating.[120] Writing our story with love is an art; and like the mastery of any art, it requires practice. Humans can only find fulfilment when they construct their world in this way. A person who lives in such a world finds happiness everywhere, in everything he or she says and does. Love without self-interest is the highest expression of relating.

Suppression of the higher self hardens our heart and covers our capacity to love purely. It is the most pervasive kind of self-inflicted violence. Indeed, it is the root of all other forms of aggression. Violence to others is always preceded by violence to oneself. It is like picking up hot coals to throw at someone else. We are always the one who gets burned first.

The highest faculty of the human being is not his rationality, but his capacity to emerge from violence and to love purely, without self-interest. Erich Fromm was right: "Thought can only lead us to the knowledge that it cannot give us the ultimate answer."[121] What we need is not thinking, but *good thinking*. Good thinking is thinking in the service of love. Otherwise, we will turn our very powers of thought against ourselves – as we have done for millennia.

∉ SELFLESS GIVING ∉

There is an ancient custom in India, now almost forgotten, that on your birthday or your wedding day you don't receive gifts: you give them. So on the day my wife and I were married in India by our teacher, we arranged for *kheer*, a delicious rice pudding, to be made for ten thousand pilgrims from the small villages of Bengal. Large fire pits several feet deep were dug into the clay ground and lined with bricks to create blistering stoves. The rice pudding was cooked on these stoves in gigantic metal woks, each the size of a small living room. Several muscular men would stir the bubbling *kheer* with enormous wooden paddles that resembled the oars of an ancient ship. We then helped distribute this to thousands of people.

I cannot express how deeply satisfying and rewarding that simple act was. Our wedding ceremony was modest, and the day did not feel like it was all about us. Instead, it was a day for overcoming our own narcissism and reaffirming our joint intent to use this life for the good of others. This in itself made it one of the most memorable days of my life.

The ability to love actually depends on our capacity to emerge from narcissism.[122] Real love is not to love people because they will love me for loving them. By putting ourselves in the centre, we try to make all things serve us. We transform others into commodities for our own enjoyment. We treat others as lifeless things. Thus, we live in isolation. When we try to make all things serve us, we find ourselves utterly alone.

Overcoming our separateness, leaving the prison of our aloneness, is our deepest need as human beings.[123] We overcome our isolation when we live for others rather than for ourselves – when we no longer reduce our brothers and sisters to the level of objects for our own enjoyment. When we give selflessly of ourselves and cast aside all measure of gain, we gain beyond all measure. Indeed, true love does not serve any purpose except itself. As my teacher explained:

> Love has nothing to take but everything to give. … We want to be completely selfless in our dealings, and for this we have the example of the tree, which gives its bark, roots, fruits, leaves, wood and shade. The tree offers everything to others with no expectation of remuneration. Why can't we human beings be so selfless?[124]

Many people are afraid of not being loved; but our real, though usually unconscious, fear is that of loving. We are afraid to let people into our heart. This is reflected in the discomfort we feel in the simple act of giving and receiving. When people buy gifts, they often perform a kind of calculus to match the value of their relationships with the value of the gifts they purchase. Likewise, they often take out their mental calculators when they receive gifts.[125]

When I was living in India as a monk, I one day thanked the senior monk of the temple monastery. I remember the confused expression on his face. He didn't say anything, but he seemed almost slightly hurt. When we say "thank you", often we do so as a form of repayment, to nullify what we perceive as an existing debt. Our polite thanking sometimes serves not to let people into our heart, but to keep them at a distance. Through immediate repayment, we often hope to avoid, or minimize, our connection with others. Thus, even our thanking can at times be a way of setting up barriers to loving others.[126]

Most people give to receive. We are polite and helpful because it suits us or benefits us, or because it looks bad not to be. But giving is the highest expression of potency. It is an expression of our aliveness. When we give, we are giving of ourselves. We are giving of the most precious thing we have – our life energy.

⚡ WHAT DESTROYS OR OPPOSES LOVE ⚡

In India, the goddess of selfless love is known as Shri Radha. Her fair complexion is said to resemble saffron that has been ground upon a slab of pure gold. Her dress is the colour of the rising sun. She is the supreme goddess.[127] The Sanskrit word for "disrespect" is *aparadha* – literally, "against Radha". In other words, it is that thought or behaviour that causes Shri Radha, the goddess of love, to leave that place.[128] Love cannot bear to remain in a place where there is any form of violence.

Most people's ability to love is diminished by a lifetime of habits of violence. It's exceptionally rare to find someone who is truly non-violent. When we indulge in violence, we harden our heart and make it impossible to love.

In setting out the Dharma Code, the *Bhagavata Purana* states that in the present age, Non-violence is destroyed by a loss of discrimination and control induced by intoxication.[129]

This includes the intoxication of success or fame.[130] It dulls the finer sentiments of empathy and compassion, making one oblivious or callous to the suffering of others. As the fourteenth-century teacher Shri Vira-Raghavacharya explains in relation to the Dharma Code, "A person affected by intoxication does not notice the suffering of others, and therefore lacks compassion."[131]

In my own life, it took a lot of suffering before I could genuinely begin appreciating the pain of others. The ability to do so is essential for living the principle of Non-violence. Since Non-violence is the most important dimension of Dharma, the *Bhagavata Purana* explains:

> If one is unhappy to see the distress of other living beings and happy to see their happiness, one's Dharma is recognized as imperishable by great personalities of virtuous renown.[132]

Notes

103. Mahatma Gandhi, *My Non-violence* (1960), p. 225.

104. The Dharma principle of *ahimsa* has its origins in the ancient Vedas. For example, it appears in the *Taittiriya Samhita* (5.2.8.7) of the *Yajur Veda*, the *Kapisthala Katha Samhita* (31.11) of the *Yajur Veda*, and several times in the *Shatapatha Brahmana*. It also appears in the *Chandogya Upanishad* (3.17.4 and 8.15.1), which prohibits violence against all living beings. In the *Mahabharata* and other Dharma texts, the Sanskrit word *anrishamsya* (non-cruelty) is frequently used instead of *ahimsa*.

105. *Ahimsa paramo dharma*: "Non-violence is the highest duty" (*Mahabharata*, Vana-parva, 207.74; Drona-parva, 192.38).

106. *Udana-varga*, 5.18.

107. Rabbi Hillel, first century BCE (*Talmud Bavli* [*Babylonian Talmud*], Tractate Shabbos, Folio 31a [1996]). See also Leviticus, 19:18.

108. Luke 6:31 (New Revised Standard Version). See also Matthew 7:12 and 22:39 ("You shall love your neighbour as yourself").

109. *Hadith of al-Nawawi*, 13.

110. *Analects of Confucius*, 15.24; in S. Leys (ed.), *The Analects of Confucius* (1997).

111. *Mahabharata*, 5.1517. Similar statements can also be found in *Panchatantra*, 3.102–3; *Mahabharata*, 5.39.57; and *Vikrama-charita*, 13.2.

112. Mahatma Gandhi, *Gandhi: All Men Are Brothers* (2004), p. 160.

113. For instance, see B. K. S. Iyengar, *Astadala Yogamala*, Vol. 2 (2001), p. 38.

114. The first teaching in the Bhakti tradition is Non-violence. For example, see the story of the hunter Mrigari in the *Skanda Purana*, which is included in Chapter 12 of this book. Non-violence is also the first instruction of yoga. For instance, Patanjali places it first in his list of *yamas*, or restraints. According to the Bhakti tradition, love beyond self-interest is our natural, innate state, which is covered over by ignorance (*avidya*). This ignorance takes shape as innumerable patterns of exploitation and violence. Progress in Bhakti-yoga, the yoga of devotion, leads naturally to a softening of the heart and a genuine love and compassion for all living beings. See *Bhagavata Purana*, 3.25.21 and 11.7.38, as well as Shri Rupa Goswami, *Shri Bhakti-rasamrita-sindhu*, 1.41. See also *Shri Chaitanya-charitamrita*, Madhya, 22.147 and 24.273, quoting the *Skanda Purana*.

115. Jalal al-Din Rumi and Coleman Barks et al., *The Essential Rumi* (2004), p. 36.

116. Erich Fromm, *The Art of Loving* (1995), p. 2–3.

117. Corinne Podger, "Quarter of Mammals 'Face Extinction'", BBC News [website], 21 May 2002.

118. Marsha Walton, "Study: Only 10 Percent of Big Ocean Fish Remain", CNN [website], 14 May 2003.

119. Charles Duhigg, *The Power of Habit: Why We Do What We Do in Life and Business* (2012), p. 92.

120. Chapter 12 will explain the process for developing pure love in the Bhakti tradition, which is to make one's every act an offering of love to Vishnu, the root of all things.

121. Erich Fromm, *The Art of Loving* (1995), pp. 60–61.

122. Ibid., pp. 92 and 94–95.

123. Ibid., p. 8.

124. Shrila B. V. Narayan Goswami, lecture, Odessa (Ukraine), 22 September 2002. See also *Bhagavata Purana*, 10.22.33–35.

125. See Sophie Chevalier and Anne Monjaret, "Getting Gifting", *Scientific American Mind*, Vol. 16, No. 4 (December 2005), p. 13.

126. The polite formula "thank you" serves a surprisingly complex set of functions that underscore the transactional and impersonal nature of contemporary Western society. "Thank you" frequently has very little to do with gratitude, whether or not the thanker actually feels grateful. When the formula "thank you" is used as a return gift out of a sense of indebtedness, the return gift serves the function of erasing or at least reducing indebtedness, and thereby helps restore an equilibrium of power. This explains the phrase "I owe you one" as an alternative way of saying "thank you". Interestingly, the practice of saying a phrase or formula equivalent to "thank you" was almost non-existent in ancient India (Raja Ram Mehrotra, "Verbalization of Polite Behaviour in Indian English", in *The Third International Symposium on Language and Linguistics* [1992], p. 967). This helps explain why verbalization of gratitude is very common in Indian families with a Western lifestyle, while very rare in orthodox Hindu families.

127. See "Shri Radha-Kripa-Kataksha-Stava-Raja" (spoken by Shiva to Gauri in the *Urdhvamnaya-tantra*) and "Shri Radhikashtakam" by Shrila Rupa Goswami, as well as other Sanskrit prayers and poems. Shri Radha is the eternal paramour of Shri Krishna. Chapter 12 will explain the process for developing selfless love in the Bhakti tradition.

128. *Apagata radha yasmat iti aparadha*, "*Aparadha* is that by which Shri Radha is lost to us". The Bhakti tradition recognizes disrespect to all that is sacred. This includes other living beings, known as *jiva-aparadha*. A novice in Bhakti-yoga is one who performs worship and sacred rituals in the temple but who disrespects others (see *Bhagavata Purana*, 11.2.47).

129. *Bhagavata Purana*, 1.17.24. See the commentaries to this verse by Shri Vamsidhara ("Bhavartha-dipika-prakasha") Shri Vira-Raghavacharya ("Bhagavata-chandrika"), Shri

Vijayadhvaja Tirtha ("Pada-ratnavali"), Shrila Jiva Goswami ("Krama-sandarbha") and Shrila Vishvanatha Chakravarti Thakura ("Sarartha-darshini").

130. The *Bhagavata Purana*, for example, refers to the "intoxication of opulence" (*shri-mada*), as in 10.10.7 and 10.10.13. ("Opulence" can refer to strength, fame, wealth, knowledge, beauty or renunciation.)

131. Shri Vira-Raghavacharya, "Bhagavata-chandrika", 1.17.24.

132. *Bhagavata Purana*, 6.10.9. See also *Mahabharata*, 5.36.16.

CHAPTER 8

DISCIPLINE

W HEN CARBON, the element that makes up ordinary coal, undergoes intense heat and crushing pressures in the depths of the earth, it transforms into a diamond. To reveal our dormant potential, to manifest our purpose, similarly requires "heat", or intensity. The Rishis expressed this fourth dimension of Dharma using the Sanskrit word *tapas* – which means, literally, "heat".

Tapas refers to ardent, one-pointed, self-transcending drive. It is self-discipline or austerity willingly undertaken to manifest our purpose, which now exists only as an unexpressed potential. The sages say *tapas* transforms into potency.[133] In other words, someone who goes through the fire of Discipline emerges more effulgent and potent as a result. We see this quite clearly with athletes, for instance, when they emerge from months of intense, rigorous training. Their ability to say "no" to the demands of the mind and senses gives them a kind of unearthly mental strength. What athletes accomplish on the sports field, we too can achieve on the field of life.

Tapas has immense creative power. According to ancient legend, *tapas* was the first word spoken at the dawn of creation.[134] In other words, it's impossible to create anything of value without some level of Discipline. It is said that Discipline invokes a power greater than ourselves; it summons the gods, who bestow upon us strength, learning, wealth or whatever other gifts we desire most.

⁂ THE "DESIRE TREE" ⁂

India has fascinated travellers and kings for millennia. In the thirteenth century, Marco Polo described a sixty-mile fishery of pearls in the gulf of a bay like none he had ever seen. It belonged to a king from the "race of the moon". Local divers, accustomed to dive from their earliest infancy, would fearlessly descend to a depth of five to ten fathoms, in search of oysters containing lustrous round pearls, "sufficient to supply the demands of all countries".[135]

Marco Polo explains that the gulf was infested by blood-hungry sharks. To avoid the unrestrained ravages of these animals, the pearl merchants would employ "enchanters belonging to a class of Brahmans, who, by means of their diabolical art, have the power of constraining and stupifying these fish so as to prevent them from doing mischief... The enchanters are likewise profound adepts in the art of fascinating all kinds of beasts and birds."[136] Whatever one might think of this account of shark-charmers ("binders of sharks"), there is a different legend from India, equally strange and wonderful, that I have some experience of myself.

Certain venerable trees in India are believed to be *kalpa-vrikshas*, or "desire trees", capable of making dreams come true.[137] When I was twelve years old, on my first visit to India I discovered a tree that had this reputation in the region. It was a dark, gnarled tamal tree, its blackish branches twisting into the sky. Out of its dark trunk also emerged a large white branch, so that half the tree was black and the other half white.

As I approached the venerable tree, I had the strange sense it was watching me. Locals believe that Rishis from the ancient world sometimes assume the form of these trees to perfect their meditation. With a simple heart, I folded my hands together and circumambulated the tree four times, in the customary way of showing respect in India. I then placed my forehead on the tree's trunk, closed my eyes and made my wish. A week later I returned to England and forgot about the incident.

My family had only recently moved to England and I was now at a new school, Soar Valley College. I had been out of school for several years, and the other students in my year were therefore well ahead of me in all key subjects. When I first arrived at the school, I was sometimes disruptive in lessons. Now, I decided to apply myself. So when my friends were watching their favourite TV programmes or playing football in the park, I focused with great Discipline on improving my English and mastering the British system of maths. I even took up German as an additional GCSE subject, through lessons in my lunch break.

By mid-June 1991, I had completed all of my exams and submitted all my coursework. Then, in the last week of August, an envelope addressed to me arrived in the post. My heart raced as I realized it contained my final exam results. At that moment, a memory returned to me, like a small, colourful bird returning after a long winter. I remembered pressing my head against the bark of the gnarled tamal tree many years ago. It was a petty wish. I had asked for only "A" grades in my studies – and to make it specific, I had picked the round number ten, off the top of my head. As I held the letter, I was sure my wish had come true. I opened the envelope and there it was: an unbroken column of A's. I counted them. There were ten.

Despite the seemingly magical nature of this event early in my life, it actually taught me the value of *tapas*, or Discipline. This is what had made the outcome possible. One Dharma text therefore advises, "As one cannot get oil from sesame seeds without pressing them, even if fate is favourable, one should not give up hard work."[138] Dharma, the phenomenon of "lift" in our life, is impossible without Discipline. An aircraft may have the finest engineered wings, carefully tested in a wind tunnel to be as aerodynamic as possible. But those perfect wings will be entirely futile and never achieve lift if they are not powered forward at sufficient speed. We can liken the velocity necessary for lift to Discipline, the fourth dimension of Dharma.

⚮ LIVING WITH A BURNING HEART ⚮

Discipline is about subjecting ourselves, willingly, to fire. However, "fire" here doesn't mean pressure exerted on us by others against our will. Rather, it means the fire of spontaneity and passion that burns in the inner chamber of our being. When that fire of life burns with fierce intensity, it can manifest our purpose. It can even make the impossible possible. But if we are continually avoiding inner intensity in our life, we will never become the diamond we are capable of becoming.

When we live with a burning heart, whatever we do feels effortless. Our life becomes an authentic expression of who we are. Living is no longer a burden but a privilege.

In nature, everything happens effortlessly, without straining. The rivers don't work against their own process as they flow to the sea. The grass doesn't strain to grow. We, however, are always straining. We work against ourselves. Discipline is therefore not simply about doing a lot, but about doing what accords with the law of our being. What we do then enlivens us, rather than saps us of strength. It's easy to find people who are striving ceaselessly; but it's rare to find someone who is able to act from a place of vitality and discernment.

The simplest definition of Discipline is to give our very best by body, words and mind.[139] If we are not burning with fire within us, we can give our best only for a day or two. We will not be able to sustain what we do. It's therefore important to protect the fire of life. We need to guard it against forces that would stifle and suffocate it. Thus, Discipline requires Purity, which is to nurture and protect our world. The oxygen of this fire within us is inner freedom. When we cultivate inner freedom, the unobstructed fire of life begins to burn fiercely.

Discipline manifests the best in us. When we truly follow the Dharma principle of Discipline, we listen to our burning heart without pride or fear of failure. Human beings are capable of extraordinary things. If we really want to do something, we always find a way. If we don't, we find an excuse.

Sometimes, awareness of death, or the short duration of our life, helps us put the dimensions of Dharma into practice. As Steve Jobs, co-founder and former CEO of Apple Computer and Pixar Animation Studios, put it:

> Remembering that I'll be dead soon is the most important tool I've ever encountered to help me make the big choices in life. Because almost everything – all external expectations, all pride, all fear of embarrassment or failure – these things just fall away in the face of death, leaving only what is truly important. Remembering that you are going to die is the best way I know to avoid the trap of thinking you have something to lose. You are already naked. There is no reason not to follow your heart.[140]

Three years ago, my younger brother David was diagnosed with stage-four cancer. He was just thirty-one years old. The disease had spread rapidly through the lymphatic system, invading his abdomen, lungs and other organs. The malignant growth in his abdomen was the size of a large grapefruit. David was immediately put on the most intensive chemotherapy treatment available today. His chance of survival, the doctors said, was 50 per cent. Today, after an operation that nearly cost David his life, David is still alive and well. He is also transformed: he lives every day as if it is the only day he has left in this world. In other words, he now lives with presence and intensity.

Every three months, my brother travels to London for a cancer screening at the hospital. He can never be sure what the tests will reveal. Like David, we too actually don't know how much time we have left. Anything can happen. This awareness suddenly makes life *extremely valuable*. There is not a moment to waste or to postpone.

We tend to waste a lot of precious life-energy. Every second we spend upset about something is a second of happiness we can never get back. Whenever we hold an angry or anxious thought, it occupies the space of a happy thought. It captures the only real estate we truly have in life – the present moment. When we live with a burning heart, life is simply too precious to fritter away.

⚹ FINDING THE BEST WITHIN US – AND THINKING AND ACTING FROM THAT PLACE ⚹

As mentioned previously, Discipline needs to be understood in the light of the other three Dharma principles. We will therefore consider further what Discipline looks like when combined with Truth, Purity and Non-violence.

In our anxiety-ridden culture, a diminished, failing perceptual world is the norm. It is what we encounter most regularly when we look into the windows of other people's lives; or when we dare candidly to examine our own. All too often we discover a shallow shop-window of appearances and borrowed dreams. It's rare to find a world that exudes authenticity to self, gratitude, love, kindness and joy.

When we are controlled by our conditioned reactions, our world is ordinary. Fear, anger, jealousy, egotism: these are all ordinary. We see them all about us – in the affronted ego, the need to be right, the thirst for compliments. When we cultivate qualities that are extraordinary, we begin to inhabit an extraordinary world. We begin to invoke Dharma through the practice of Discipline, or "right effort". One who crosses beyond fear, confusion and lamentation crosses into the exceptional.

Discipline is the inner fire that forges transformation in our life. Each of the four dimensions of Dharma carries several layers of meaning. When we master one level it opens up a still-deeper wisdom. Discipline isn't just about doing a lot and not giving up. When combined with the other Dharma principles, it's also about acting from the best place within us. We can work very hard, but if the direction is wrong then we have simply accentuated or enlarged the problems of life.

The first step, therefore, is to locate ourselves and find the right direction.[141] This is part of the commitment to Truth, the first dimension of Dharma. Right action has two dimensions: effort and direction. Before applying any effort, we need to be sure about our direction. There are ways of acting that free us and there are ways of acting that bind us. So many of us act from a position of fear, regret or confusion, and yet we expect our actions to deliver life-nurturing and fulfilling outcomes. This is impossible.

Often we neglect quality of being in our relentless effort to get things done. We want to cover mileage each day of our life. But imagine two people who set out to sea, one in a rowing boat and the other in a large steamer. The man in the steamer will be shovelling coal into the steamer, working hard. He will cover a 100 miles in the time the man in the rowing boat covers just 10. But if those 10 miles are in the right direction and the 100 miles are in the wrong direction, then the man in the rowing boat is up to 110 miles better off.

Thus, it's important never to act from a negative place, such as when we are angry or overcome by frustration or the urge to dominate. This is when we will most want to act. But we cannot trust ourselves here. The negativity will contaminate everything we do. It's wise to act only from the best within us, and our best is what our actions and their results will be imbued with.

Ultimately, what we send out is what we attract back into our lives. Anger begets anger; hate breeds hate; love inspires love; laughter almost always gives rise to laughter; humility engenders humility; and honesty tends to provoke honesty. The force we send out is the effect we receive back.

⚘ TREATING OUR BODY AS A TEMPLE ⚘

Importantly, my teacher taught me that Discipline is not about abusing or torturing our body.[142] In the West, we tend to connect self-mastery with pain, on the misguided belief that there is no gain without pain. But self-mastery is not about punishing ourselves. It's about breaking free from punishing patterns of thought and behaviour. It is about caring for our body, mind and heart to such an extent that we function at our optimum, so we may be of service in the world to the best of our ability.

Our physical body, although temporary, is a vehicle by which we manifest our purpose in this world. It is the instrument through which we express our potential. It is therefore extremely valuable. Looking after our body and mind is therefore the first step to practising Discipline in our life. It is a precondition to cultivating Dharma.

Fruit farmers know that to get the best quality and quantity from their trees, they need to provide their trees with optimal conditions for growth. They therefore pamper the trees in their orchard. Race horse trainers apply the same principle too. They pamper their horses. They give them the best food, making sure not to feed them too much or too little. They exercise their horses daily and praise them often, continually pushing them a little harder when they reach a threshold. Human beings are no different. For the human body to work at its optimum, it requires optimal conditions.

Thus, Discipline also means taking time for healthy and peaceful meals and getting the rest we need. As the

Bhagavad-gita explains, it means not eating too much or too little, and not sleeping too much or too little.[143] It is about finding the optimal balance for physical and mental well-being, while freeing oneself from inner obstacles and addictions.

Most of all, we tend to punish the body through our thoughts. We metabolize our thoughts and give them sanctuary in our body. We wonder whether we are good enough. We forget that we, the conscious self, are the origin of all value in our perceptual "kingdom". We become plagued by self-doubt, self-pity and self-hatred. For many people, life seems just like a hopeless fight against themselves. We become our own worst enemy, sometimes becoming repulsive even to ourselves. Discipline is about not falling victim to such defeating thoughts, and being kind to ourselves. We are a child of the universe – no less than the trees, rivers and stars. We have a right to be here.

⚡ MOST POWERFUL IS SHE WHO HAS HERSELF IN HER OWN POWER ⚡

Someone unfamiliar with the Dharma principle of Discipline might think of Discipline as coercive or restrictive. But Discipline is actually a manifestation of human potency, brought about by breaking free from the coercion of the mind and senses. Discipline generates great freedom in life. Stephen Covey explains:

> Most people equate discipline with an absence of freedom.
> In fact, the opposite is true. Only the disciplined are truly free.
> The undisciplined are slaves to moods, appetites and passions.

> Can you play the piano? I can't. I don't have the freedom
> to play the piano. I never disciplined myself. ... What
> about the freedom to forgive, to ask forgiveness? What
> about the freedom to love unconditionally, to be a light,
> not a judge – a model, not a critic? Think of the discipline
> involved in these. Discipline comes from being "discipled"
> to a person or a cause.[144]

In the West, many people seem to suffer more from their mind than from their body. This is because we struggle to discipline the mind. From the moment we wake up to the moment we fall asleep, the mind is continually speaking, speaking, speaking. We have become so used to our "internal dialogue" that we no longer question it.

What does the mind tell us? Usually, it is inventing needless drama in our life. It either wants or it worries. The mind tells us, "I'm upset" or "I'm anxious", and we internalize this and believe it unquestioningly. If we hurt our elbow or knee, we would never say "I'm a hurt elbow" or "I'm a grazed knee". But when the mind declares "I'm upset", we identify with it and react to it immediately. It affects the entire course of our day. We spend the rest of the day punishing ourselves with angry or anxious thoughts.

The workings of the mind are a repetitive cycle; the more we believe that something is true, the more our mind will create circumstances to make it so. The most powerful time to control what unfolds from our actions is at their very inception, when they are fledgling thoughts. We are each able to be aware of the workings of our thoughts, as a detached observer. This gives us the power to alter thinking, and thereby to affect our own reality. The ability to observe the mind dispassionately and to still it, is known in India as yoga.[145]

Someone who has conquered the mind in this way has conquered all things. In the *Bhagavad-gita*, Krishna, the "master of all mystics", tells Arjuna: "For a person who has conquered his mind, the mind is a friend; but for one who has failed to do so, his mind works against him, just like an enemy."[146] The mind has the power to elevate us and also to destroy us, depending upon the habits we adopt in our life.

Through Discipline, we transform the mind into an engine that elevates us. Discipline generates great power through focus, so that we may achieve anything in life. In doing so, it builds character and leads to self-respect. As Abraham J. Heschel observed, "Self-respect is the fruit of discipline, the sense of dignity grows with the ability to say No to oneself."[147]

⁘ ALEXANDER THE GREAT MEETS THE RISHIS OF INDIA ⁘

Once, Alexander the Great was marching through a province in northern India with his many soldiers and entourage. In a meadow he chanced upon a group of Rishis, or sages, who would meet there to discuss philosophy. Upon seeing Alexander and his powerful army passing by, these venerable sages stamped the ground with their feet and then paid no further interest.

Intrigued, Alexander asked them through his interpreter what they meant by this odd behaviour. One of the Rishis replied, "King Alexander, every human can possess only as much of the earth's surface as they are standing on. You are human like the rest of us, except that, fuelled by ambition, you have come very far from your home to be a nuisance to yourself and to all others. Ah, well! In a short time you will be dead, and then you will own just as much of the earth as is needed to bury you."

Alexander was struck by these words, and expressed his approval to the Rishis. But the Roman general and historian Arrian, writing during the rule of Emperor Antoninus, observes that Alexander's conduct was always the exact opposite of the wisdom he professed to admire. Arrian writes, "One must admit, then, that Alexander was not wholly a stranger to the loftier flights of philosophy; but the fact remains that he was, to an extraordinary degree, the slave of ambition."[148]

Alexander the Great died a young man having accomplished many feats, having travelled all the way into India, but never having completed the most important journey of all – the inner journey. Despite Alexander's great outward power, he had not achieved true freedom. Having conquered the world without, he had not mastered the world within, and thus he lacked true freedom. He was a servant of his own uncontrolled mind and senses.

To be inwardly free means to have conquered the mind, the king of the senses. This requires Discipline. "When mental energy is allowed to follow the line of least resistance, and to fall into easy channels," James Allen wrote, "it is called weakness; when it is gathered, focused, and forced into upward and difficult directions, it becomes power; and this concentration of energy and acquisition of power is brought about by means of self-control."[149]

Notes

133. *Tapas* transforms into *tejas*, or potency. Rishis and kings of the ancient world would engage in *tapas* to increase their potency, especially before beginning any difficult undertakings. All practices of *tapas* involved the resolute and voluntary restraint of the mind and senses.

134. *Bhagavata Purana*, 2.9.6. See also *Bhagavata Purana*, 2.9.24.

135. Marco Polo, *The Travels of Marco Polo, a Venetian, in the Thirteenth Century* (1818), p. 625.

136. Ibid.

137. The ancient texts of India refer to such trees, known as *kalpa-vriksha* or *kalpa-taru* (e.g. *Bhagavata Purana*, 1.1.3; *Brahma-samhita*, 5.29). My teacher has explained that many of the trees in the sacred land of Vrindavan can fulfil wishes.

138. *Hitopadesha*, 1.32. Similarly, verse 1.30 of the *Hitopadesha* states, "As a chariot cannot move on one wheel, so fate cannot yield results without endeavour." Translations from Satya Narayana Dasa, *The Hitopadesa of Sri Narayana Pandita*, Book One (1997).

139. The *Bhagavad-gita* defines *tapas* in three verses: 17.14 (*tapas* of the body), 17.15 (*tapas* of speech) and 17.16 (*tapas* of the mind).

140. Steve Jobs, "Steve Jobs: How to live before you die", Stanford University commencement speech (12 June 2005).

141. This is why in many traditions in India, including the Bhakti tradition, practitioners will engage in meditation in the early hours of the day. This awakens our higher nature, which we then carry into the day. Before beginning any important endeavour, including the transmitting of wisdom, practitioners will perform a *mangalacarana*, or "auspicious invocation", which fosters a state of being that leads to optimal outcomes.

142. The *Bhagavad-gita* (17.5–6 and 17.19) decries any form of *tapas* that tortures the body.

143. For instance, see *Bhagavad-gita*, 6.16–17.

144. Stephen R. Covey, *The 8th Habit: From Effectiveness to Greatness* (2005), p. 74.

145. *Bhagavad-gita*, 2.48: *samatvam yoga uchyate* ("yoga is evenness [of mind]").

146. Ibid., 6.6. In the texts of India, Krishna is frequently referred to as the "master of all mystics" (e.g. *Bhagavad-gita*, 18.78; *Bhagavata Purana*, 2.8.20, 3.4.25, 8.3.27 and 10.69.38).

147. Abraham J. Heschel, T*he Insecurity of Freedom* (1967), p. 44.

148. Arrian, *The Campaigns of Alexander* (1971), pp. 349–50.

149. James Allen, *The Life Triumphant: Mastering the Heart and Mind* (2007), p. 46.

III

APPLYING THE DHARMA CODE IN EVERYDAY LIFE

CHAPTER 9

BREATHING LIFE INTO THE DHARMA CODE

"DHARMA DESTROYS THOSE WHO DESTROY IT. DHARMA PROTECTS THOSE WHO PROTECT IT."

– Emperor Yudhisthira[150]

SOME 1,500 YEARS AGO, the physician of the Emperor of Persia came into possession of a valuable book from India that held the secret of a *rasayana*, an elixir for raising the dead. The book explained how to prepare the elixir, by combining rare herbs that grew on the mountains of India. Eager to procure this *rasayana*, the Emperor dispatched his physician with a retinue of men on the long and perilous journey to India, bearing valuable gifts.

Crossing the Khyber Pass into India, the physician was well-received by the king who ruled the Himalayan foothills. The king engaged his best scholars to help the physician gather the various mountain herbs he needed. The physician combined these herbs in different ways and sprinkled them on to corpses; but no combination could raise a person from the dead. After repeated failures, the physician concluded at last with a heavy heart that the claims in the Hindu book must be false.

It troubled the physician greatly to return to Persia empty-handed and disappoint his Emperor. Some village elders therefore advised him to seek out a specific Rishi, who had himself searched hard for the same elixir in his youth. Perhaps he would be able to help.

The physician found this venerable Rishi, who lived in a Himalayan cave, and told him about his troubles.

"Don't be discouraged," the Rishi said. "The *rasayana* exists, but its purpose is not to raise the dead at the end of their life. It is to raise the dead during the course of their life."

The physician looked bewildered, so the Rishi explained: "Many people are afraid of death, but they never ask themselves whether they have yet truly begun living. Have they manifested the powerful Dharma monarch within them? Do they have sovereignty over their kingdom, which is their life, or are they asleep to life and simply playing out habits they never chose? Is their life a reflection of their lower self or their higher self? Death during life is far more tragic than death at the end of life. The *rasayana* you seek is intended to cure this first, and more serious, type of death."

The physician was himself a student of sacred lore, and he understood these words of the Rishi. He was now hardly able to contain himself. "Do you know the secret of this *rasayana*?" he asked. "What is this elixir, and how is it prepared?"

"To conceal the *rasayana*, the account of how to prepare it has been written in the form of an allegory. The Himalayan mountains are the Rishis of great wisdom and high character. The medicinal mountain herbs are their various writings on the subject of Dharma. And the *rasayana* is the wisdom of Dharma that may be extracted from these writings. That wisdom, when applied, is so potent that it generates great vitality in a person's life and manifests their highest potential. It raises from the dead the Dharma king or queen in each of us. We then rise from our death-like slumber. We come to see a lifetime not as the amount of time in our life, but as the amount of life in our time. There is no limit to the potency of one who lives in accord with the principles of Dharma."

The Rishi thereupon directed the physician to a collection of Dharma teachings specifically for monarchs that was in the king's personal possession. These teachings, he said, are the medicinal herbs the physician needed to collect.

The Himalayan king was reluctant to reveal the Dharma teachings to the physician; but at last he relented, allowing the physician to view the manuscript only in his presence. Every day, the physician would read from the book, but only as much as he was able to commit to heart. In the night, the physician would write what he had read and send this to the Persian Emperor in secret dispatches. He persevered until finally he received a reply to his letters, which read:

"The sea of knowledge has reached us."

The physician now returned to Persia, where he was personally received by the great Emperor. The compendium of Dharma teachings was safely placed in the Persian royal treasury. It is said that no unqualified person ever beheld it.

In gratitude for these teachings, the Persian Emperor gave the physician the key of his treasury-house and asked him to take from it anything he wished.

I learned about this story from an old man in India, who had in turn heard it from his grandfather. A version of this same account, I later discovered, is also to be found in *The Book of the Kings*, written for the Samani princes of Persia more than a thousand years ago.[151]

Like the physician, I had travelled halfway around the world on a journey into India. I knew that to extract the *rasayana* of Dharma from the medicinal writings of the ancients, I would need the help of a true, enlightened Rishi. I met such a wise Rishi in 1991, and apprenticed with him for sixteen years. Gradually, I learned from him about the hidden teachings for Dharma kings, and about the four types of medicinal herbs for preparing the *rasayana* of Dharma – Truth, Purity, Non-violence and Discipline. But having collected the ingredients, how was the *rasayana* to be administered? The *rasayana* of Dharma must somehow flow through human veins and be embodied in our person. If we simply gather the ingredients but don't actually drink the *rasayana*, we will not raise the monarch within us.

⚒ THE LAST LESSON FROM MY TEACHER ⚒

During my training as a monk, I memorized more than three-thousand verses of wisdom from the sacred texts and poetry of India. In the morning, my teacher would have me and the other students recite to him the Sanskrit verses we had learned the previous day and explain their meaning in detail. He would correct our mistakes, and then himself elucidate the deeper teachings of these verses.

One morning my teacher turned to me and asked, "Can you tell me the reason why I request you to memorize these verses?" He gazed at me with his deep blue eyes, which resembled the sea and seemed to look directly into the deepest corners of my soul.

I was caught off guard by the simplicity of the question. "This particular verse?" I asked, trying to buy a moment.

"I give you so many verses to memorize. Why?"

"So that we can have a proper understanding and grounding in the principles of Truth?" I proffered somewhat timidly. It sounded a sophisticated enough reply, I thought.

"So that we can see where we are?" another student suggested.

"The reason I ask you to learn these verses is so that you will perfectly practise them in your life," my teacher said simply. "At that time the fruit of learning will manifest. Remembering alone will not suffice. Whatever you memorize, try to practise in your life."

My teacher understood that I was trapped in the realm of concepts. I could ponder deeper truths all my life, and even explain them eloquently, but until I actually applied them in my life, they were as good as useless to me. In other words, after understanding the principles of Dharma intellectually, I would need to breathe life into them. To do this, I would need to embody them in my life.

My teacher then told us the story of a great mentor named Dronacharya, who gave all his warrior students a lesson consisting of a single statement: "Always speak Truth." The following day, Dronacharya asked his students if they had retained the lesson.

"Yes, I have memorized it. I have learned it," they declared. However, Yudhisthira, destined to become a great Dharma king, remained silent.

"No, I have not retained the lesson," Yudhisthira said at last.

Dronacharya asked Yudhisthira why that was.

"I have not yet made that lesson part of my character. When I do this, then it can be said I have retained it."

Dronacharya was immensely pleased. He told all of his students that in uttering Truth, Yudhisthira had demonstrated that he had indeed retained the lesson, while the others had not.

The wisdom verses I had learned held immense potency, like magical arrows. I had collected more than three-thousand arrows in my quiver. But these shafts would be of no avail if I did not perfect the mantra, or incantation, for releasing them on the battlefield of life. To perfect the mantra for these arrows that vanquish ignorance, I needed to embody them in my life. This, I knew, was the hardest thing to do. Without it, all the wisdom verses in my possession would be of no avail when I required them most. I would be vanquished by fear, confusion and lamentation.

A few days later, as if to confirm what my teacher had

taught me, I came upon the following verse from a Dharma text for training young princes:

> Just as a lamp in the hand of a blind man cannot help him
> see, so the instructions of the sacred texts yield no fruit for
> those who do not act on them with determination.[152]

This exchange with my teacher was especially meaningful for me because it was the last direct teaching my teacher gave me before he left this world the following year.

⸙ CULTIVATING LIVING WISDOM ⸙

Humans today are supposed to be *Homo sapiens sapiens,* Latin for "man, the extremely wise"; but our wisdom is fragile and questionable. As a species, we pride ourselves on being exceptionally intelligent. But our society is frequently characterized not by wisdom but by its opposite, folly. Very few of us have what we might call "wise perception".

Homo sapiens sapiens is therefore not what we are: it's what we're still in the process of becoming. To be sure, in a few short decades we have managed to trigger climate change, kill off a large percentage of our plant and animal species, threaten the extinction of most remaining species of large mammals, and pollute the earth with plastic, chemical waste and oil spills. Human life on earth is in jeopardy not from our want of knowledge, but our want of wisdom.

I learned from my teacher that wisdom reveals itself in its living practice. This perhaps explains why so many of us know a lot, but so few are truly wise. We are reluctant to move beyond the realm of words. We accumulate ideas and add them to our vast edifice of thought, but little changes in the way we lead our lives.

Failure to apply the four principles of Dharma in any "territory" leads to systemic or structural jeopardy. If we design our life, or any other "territory", in accord with the four principles of Dharma, we can expect results that are vital, sustainable on all levels, and a manifestation of living wisdom.

Confucius compared the development of good habits to learning how to play music.[153] It requires, among other things, practice. Aristotle used a similar metaphor:

> Men become builders by building houses, and harpists by playing the harp. Similarly, we grow just by the practice of just actions, self-controlled by exercising our self-control, and courageous by performing acts of courage.[154]

The Dharma teachings are similarly perfected through practice; until that happens, they remain only good ideas.

⚘ THE WARRIOR AND THE MONK ⚘

The Dharma teachings can be put into action by just about anyone. They are not the reserve of monks. After all, the Rishis created the Dharma Code specifically for warrior kings.

Both the solitary monk and the warrior have to embody Dharma in the present moment. Each is on a personal journey, and the only advantage either may have is greater practice in applying the Dharma Code. By warrior, I mean the business executive, parent, student or other individual who is in direct engagement with the refining challenges of everyday life. Therefore, when I refer to the warrior, I almost certainly mean the reader.

The warrior who practises Dharma in fact has an important advantage over the solitary monk. The quality of our practice is not only a function of how much effort we put in, but also of the arena in which we apply the Dharma Code. The word "monk" comes from the Greek *monos*, which means "alone".[155] While many monks live together in monasteries and are in direct engagement with the world, there has always been a class of monks in India that lived in isolation in the forest or in Himalayan caves. Unlike the solitary monk, we, the warrior, are practising Dharma in the very best field of learning – the chaos of everyday life.

The *Bhagavad-gita*, a foremost Dharma text, is a dialogue between Krishna and Arjuna that takes place directly between two armies on a battlefield. This battlefield represents the chaos of everyday engagement. The warrior Arjuna's first application of the Dharma teachings he had learned was on that field, amidst the confusion of battle – just as ours will be in the swift and sometimes turbulent environment of everyday life.

Notes

150. *Mahabharata*, 3.314.128; and *Manusmriti*, 8.15.

151. The compendium of teachings referred to in this story is said to be the renowned *Panchatantra* of Vishnu Sharma, originally composed in the third century BCE. A collection of instructions for kings, the *Panchatantra* quotes extensively from the Dharma teachings found in the Puranas and Itihasas. It was translated into Pahlavi, and became known as the *Kalila*. A version of this story is found in the *Shahnameh* or *Shah-Nama* (*The Book of the Kings*), composed by the revered Persian author Ferdowsi between c. 977 and 1010 CE for the princes of the Samani Dynasty of Persia. (See Ferdowsi, *The Epic of Kings: Shah-Nama* [2011], pp. 330–334.)

152. *Hitopadesha*, 1.165. The *Hitopadesha* ("Good Instructions") is a collection of teachings for young princes composed by Vishnu Sharma on the request of King Dhavalachandra. Many of its verses can be traced to the Dharma teachings found in the Puranas and Itihasas.

153. C. Hansen, "Classical Chinese Ethics"; in P. Singer (ed.), *A Companion to Ethics* (1991), pp. 69–81.

154. Aristotle, *Nichomachean Ethics* (1962), 1103b.

155. The Greek *monos* is traceable to the Sanskrit *muni*, meaning "monk". *Muni* occurs in this sense for the first time in the *Rig Veda*, which extols the way of the lone hermits, who have withdrawn to the forest and a life of wandering. The disposition of a *muni* is *mauna*, or silence.

CHAPTER 10

Thoughts, Actions, Habits, Character

I

T WAS A FESTIVAL DAY. The temple monastery had cooked a small feast for all the locals, who streamed into the building in large numbers for the afternoon worship of Vishnu, and then sat in the open courtyard on floor mats in rows. I went to fetch the plates and bowls, which were fashioned out of large leaves woven together. They lay next to hundreds of pale cups made of river clay, which had been sun-dried and half-baked in an open fire. There is a gratifying, childlike pleasure that comes with tossing these clay cups after use and hearing the "pop!" as you watch them hit the ground and shatter into bits.

I brought down several large stacks of leaf plates. Each bundle held perhaps a hundred plates and was tightly bound up with thick, coarse string. It was impossible to pull off the string without damaging the leaf plates, so I proceeded to try to break the cord with my bare hands. Soon my hands were puffed and red, and I realized this wouldn't work. A senior monk had been watching me with some amusement.

"Breaking this string is like trying to change your character – it is very, very difficult," the monk said at last. He held the thick, coarse string in one hand and with the other gave it a little twist to reveal three thinner intertwined threads.

"These thinner threads are like the habits that make up your character. They can be broken, but it is still difficult," he continued. "But look, each of these thinner threads is made up of three further delicate fibres. These fibres are very easy to break." To demonstrate, he easily snapped one of them between the nails of his thumb and index finger.

"These delicate fibres are your individual thoughts and actions," he explained. "They combine together to create your habits. If you guard the quality of your thoughts, you can guard the quality of your actions. If you guard the quality of your actions, you can protect the quality of your habits. And if you protect the quality of your habits, you can ensure quality of character."

The guests were now all seated and it was time to begin serving the various tasty dishes the monks had cooked all morning. There was no time for further delay. The senior monk called for a knife. With a single stroke, he slashed the cords to release hundreds of leaf plates.

"The knife is the company of saints and Rishis," he said. "Simply by their words and example, they cut to pieces our accumulated habits of ignorance. By the sheer potency of their presence, they can transform a person's character."

⚜ THE SECRET, ILLICIT LOVER ⚜

Why is living in accord with Dharma so difficult? And what is the secret for applying the Dharma Code in our everyday life? There are many ways to apply the Code. I want to share with you the method that works best for me.

I have found that the secret of applying the Dharma Code actually lies in understanding how we create the "kingdom" of our life. Most of our life is a web of habits. We may not even be aware of the sheer extent of our habits. These habits are like laws. They govern our kingdom and shape its future.

When we oppose Dharma in some way, we do so at first with a single thought. This might be the thought to hurt someone, to take unfair advantage of a situation, to exert our superiority, to judge harshly. By returning to that thought and feeding it, we create a multiplicity of thoughts. Soon we find ourselves acting on our thoughts. Our actions become our habits; our habits become our character; and our character forges our destiny.

I realized that the further up in this chain I try to apply the Dharma Code, the more difficult it is. If someone's entire character is contrary to Dharma, it is extremely difficult to alter that. It is like trying to tear asunder a thick rope made of numerous interwoven threads. At the level of habits, change may be possible; but it is still fairly challenging. But at the level of thoughts, I discovered, I can operate much more freely. I can become aware of my thoughts. This is what inward-looking perception is about. I can ask myself, "Is this a Dharma thought?" If it isn't, I can let go of that thought. This is something I do all the time.

If I find myself unable to let go of a thought, I can at least stop myself from acting on that thought. To act on a thought is to cross the Rubicon, the point of no return from the realm of the mind to the realm of physicality. If I know that the act is against the Dharma Code, I can stop myself there.

Now, if I have already acted against the Dharma Code, I can try not to repeat the act and create a habit. I can also try to replace habits I may already have with Dharma habits. This is still more difficult, but it can be achieved through patience and effort. I have managed to change many habits in my own life.

A thought opposed to Dharma is like a secret, illicit lover. You exchange glances with an attractive man or woman, and this plants the seed of a thought. If you allow yourself to return to that thought, you soon find yourself thinking about that other person again and again. A single thought becomes a multiplicity of thoughts. Overwhelmed by the force of your thoughts, you helplessly find yourself acting on them. You begin to flirt with that other person and you invite them out somewhere. You buy them gifts. Before long you share an intimate experience with them, which you then long to repeat. You have now created a habit. Your habit begins to interfere with your life. You want to give it up; but you also cannot live without that other person. Before long you have destroyed your previously happy marriage, which now terminates in a divorce. Your habit has overpowered you and forged your destiny. It all started with a single thought, which you chose not to let go of.

⸕ CHOOSING DHARMA THOUGHTS ⸕

"They all have more than I do. I am not good enough. I must work harder."

"When I'm wealthy and successful, I'll be happy."

"I must show that I'm doing well. I must make myself attractive and lovable."

"I must not lose this. Without this, I am nobody."

"This person is helping me get what I want. He is my friend."

"That person is my competitor. I must overcome him. What if he gets there before I do? I mustn't allow that to happen."

These are some of the voices of the mind. We don't have such thoughts once; we repeat and reaffirm them to ourselves again and again. It is no surprise then that we also end up acting on these thoughts. Our actions gradually become habits, and we build our life with these habits.

The first step I take in applying the Dharma Code is to try to be very conscious of the thoughts I have. I discovered I can recognize when a thought is untrue, impure, aggressive or lazy. We all have this sensibility. When this happens, I try to drop that thought. I recognize that it is unhelpful. I don't always succeed in doing this, of course. But I know that rooting out what opposes Dharma when it is a mere fledgling thought is far easier than when that thought has matured into a sturdy habit and produced so many further unhelpful thoughts and desires.

I found that it's best not to get angry or upset with myself for having a negative thought. That would simply be trading one form of negativity with another. It's best simply to drop the thought and move on, treating ourselves with kindness and understanding. A negative thought cannot harm us if we don't believe in it and don't feed it.

⚞ CHOOSING DHARMA ACTIONS ⚟

If we can't help our thoughts, we can at least help our actions. Even if an action seems intelligent and reasonable, I try to consider the intent behind it. If the intent is opposed to Dharma, I try to avoid taking that action.

A few years ago I was working on a copywriting project for an investment bank located abroad. The Vice President of Marketing of the company was friendly but very challenging to work with. If I sent her a sensitive email, she would copy in half the senior managers in her reply. She also kept changing her plan of action, which made it really difficult to keep to schedules or meet deadlines. I could never be sure if she accepted responsibility for this or perhaps blamed me. Sometimes I would have to work late into the night to accommodate shifting deadlines.

One day, I decided it was time to expose the situation. After all, the principle of Truth required it. I would send her a carefully worded email about the consequences of her chaotic approach. I would copy in all the senior managers at the company. I drafted the email, and was about to hit the send button.

But I found myself hesitating. It didn't feel right. Unsure what to do, I turned to the Dharma Code. It dawned on me that while I was privileging Truth I was ignoring Non-violence. My email was polite and professional; but so often we conceal our aggression behind a veneer of professionalism. My intent was aggressive. How would the Vice President feel being exposed in this way before the other senior managers of the company? In empathizing with her, I began for the first time to recognize the many challenges she might be facing. She was new to the organization, and investment banks are known for their strong male-dominated culture. The work I was involved in was probably only a small fraction of her many responsibilities. I now found myself revising what I had earlier regarded as indubitable Truth. I realized that Truth doesn't reveal itself fully in a heart that lacks compassion.

I decided I would write to all the senior managers after all. But instead of criticizing the Vice President, I would praise her for her work. I would express my genuine appreciation for her achievements in what were sometimes fairly challenging circumstances. I cannot express what a joy it was to send that email. I also cannot express what a difference this made to our working relationship. It built trust. It made it far easier for me to speak honestly to her. It also generated immense vitality in our working relationship.

Sometimes, the principles of Dharma may initially seem to conflict with each other. If this happens, we should always privilege Non-violence, which is the highest principle.[156]

We live in an increasingly complex world, with no easy answers. We have access to more options and information than ever before, and this in itself can make decision-making more difficult. The Dharma Code is a tool for decision-making. If I have several options open to me, I use the four principles of Dharma to help me (a) rule out options that oppose Dharma and (b) select the option that best aligns with the four Dharma principles.

Many of our decisions will affect us for the rest of our life. Truth, Purity, Non-violence and Discipline are lode stars to help us navigate everyday life and make intelligent choices. The Dharma Code can help us take our life forward in a sustainable, life-enhancing way. For example, if I am considering a change of job or career, I might ask myself a few evident Dharma questions, as I weigh up a new opportunity:

Truth: *"What is working here really like, beyond initial appearances? Does the specific work or role closely fit my nature and abilities?"*

Purity: *"Is this a positive and supportive workplace or does it have a negative culture of office politics and complaining?"*

Non-violence: *"How does the company treat its people? Does it believe in profits above all else or people above all else?"*

Discipline: *"Does the work inspire me enough to go the extra mile and exceed expectations every day?"*

I consider these questions at least as important as salary, title, benefits and bonuses. Without asking them, I may make a change in my life that turns out to be unsustainable. Of course, there are times we may have no option but to take whatever work we can find. We may have a family to support, a sick child to nurse, or rising mortgage payments to make. Still, by asking these kinds of questions we make sure not to enter into anything blindly. It helps us avoid making a temporary measure a permanent life choice.

I also use the Dharma Code in a creative way to open up new pathways in my world. For instance, I will occasionally reflect on what I can do to lead a life more true to myself rather than the life others expect of me. This is a Truth question. The last time I did this, I came to see clearly what my passion in life is. My purpose, I realized, is to try to embody the teachings of my spiritual master in my own life and make those teachings accessible to contemporary readers and audiences. This awakening in itself transformed the way I lead my life.

I also regularly ask myself questions relating to the other three dimensions of Dharma:

"Am I in an environment or relationship that is not bringing out the best in me? If so, what can I do about this?"

"In what ways do I damage the planet or cause suffering to others through my everyday actions? What practical steps can I take to reduce that?"

"In what areas of my life am I lazy or undisciplined? What commitments can I make to reverse that?"

Applying the Dharma Code requires a reflective approach to life. It also requires the strength and courage to live up to what our reflective approach shows us.

⸙ CHOOSING DHARMA HABITS ⸙

I was giving a Dharma workshop recently and I asked the participants to share some of the habits they have that run counter to the Dharma Code. They indentified the following:

"I become defensive. I act as if people are attacking me, when maybe they're simply trying to help. It can make it very hard for anyone to give me feedback."

"I'm a bad listener. Usually, I'm simply waiting my turn to speak."

"I'm impatient. I do things quickly, and get really frustrated when others don't keep up."

"I'm a procrastinator. I leave things till the last minute."

"I'm insincere. I don't mean to be. Maybe it's because I want people to like me."

"I watch too much TV."

"I smoke. I also eat a lot of junk food. Sometimes I feel like a refuse bin, but I can't seem to help myself."

"I complain a lot – about my friends, my work, my life. I know deep down that I don't actually have much to complain about. It's just a habit."

Habits become an automatic and natural process for the way we live. They lead us to respond and interact in the world through a conditioned pattern of behaviours; so much so that we may not even realize the behaviours we engage in. Habits are very difficult to change. Doing so requires all the strength and cunning we can muster. It is like entering into battle: it requires a full scoping of enemy lines, careful planning, and determined execution.

The first step to overcoming harmful habits in our life is to identify them. We then also need to understand more about these habits. All habits have (1) a trigger, (2) a routine and (3) a reward.[157] The trigger, or cue, can be anything that sets off a pattern of behaviour – such as the pang of anxiety that prompts me to reach for a cigarette. If my habit is to become defensive, the trigger might be to hear any form of feedback about my work or about me. The routine is my defensiveness – becoming agitated, interrupting, denying, blaming, making excuses. The reward, or payoff, is that I feel safe. My false sense of identity in the story I have created for myself is protected. If I keep fending off any feedback through my defensive denying and blaming, I never have to change; however, the habit also prevents me from ever growing as a person.

The problem with habits is that once they are embedded, we begin following them unthinkingly as soon as we detect the trigger. Habits in our life usually cannot be eradicated. They must, instead, be replaced.[158]

If my habit is to watch TV for many hours as soon as I get home, I need something to replace that simple habit of heading for the sofa and reaching for the remote. I need to find something to fill the emptiness and agitated feelings that will arise initially. If necessary, I can even leave the trigger and the reward as they are for now, and simply replace the routine.[159] Rather than habitually pursuing a routine that is ultimately self-destructive, I can choose routines that are aligned with the Dharma Code and that yield helpful, sustainable results.

Sometimes changing a habit requires a change of environment. Certain environments are breeding grounds for certain behaviours. If my habit is to eat junk food, I may need to empty my fridge of all junk food and never bring any into the house again. If I am a smoker, it won't help if I am with smokers all day.

Letting go of a habit can feel like breaking up with a long-term lover. It can be a challenging process. It's helpful to acknowledge this and be compassionate towards ourselves.

⚡ FOLLOWING TRUTH, OUR NORTH STAR ⚡

The Dharma Code is designed to help us create Dharma habits, or habits that lead to excellence. In doing so, we emerge as *Homo sapiens sapiens*, wise humans. As Will Durant observed, "we are what we repeatedly do. Excellence, then, is not an act but a habit".[160]

To successfully apply the Dharma Code, we need to develop an unyielding commitment to Truth, our North Star. The sacred texts of India often refer to the opposite of Truth as "ignorance".[161] By this, they don't necessarily mean a lack of knowledge. Often we know what is but simply choose to *ignore it*. Ignorance is wilfully to shut our eyes to what we don't wish to recognize.

Ignorance is a terrible epidemic on this planet. Until we move out of ignorance, nothing in our life can change. The old saying that "ignorance is bliss" is plainly wrong. Ignorance will always work against us. It therefore needs to be vanquished by wisdom, or alignment with Truth. This does not require any special learning in abstruse things. What prevents us from being wise is not a lack of intellect or learning, but a lack of will.[162] Most of us are unwilling to step beyond our own illusions. Wisdom therefore has only one price – a genuine and earnest longing for it. It's as simple as that.

Supertankers and other large vessels don't change direction easily. Their rudders are as large as a tall building, and the sheer pressure exerted upon them in the water renders them almost immobile. These large rudders therefore have a small secondary rudder on them, called a "trim tab". If the ship's captain alters the direction of the small trim tab, the ship's immense rudder suddenly moves with little effort, turning a tanker that might be almost five hundred metres long in a giant arc in the water.

Like a fully loaded supertanker, we carry the cargo of a lifetime of conditioning. As humans, we have limited steering power. Wisdom is therefore possible for us only if we develop the strong desire for it. This earnest desire is the small trim tab capable of shifting our world. Without a desire for wisdom, we will go in the direction we have always gone: straight ahead.

Every time we dare to look at our own folly directly and we learn something from it, we invoke Truth. We convert folly into wisdom. Commitment to Truth, when sincere and unyielding, is a potent force in our life, vanquishing our accumulated habits of foolishness that spring from ignorance.

Notes

156. *Mahabharata*, Vana-parva, 207.74; Drona-parva, 192.38.

157. Charles Duhigg, *The Power of Habit: Why We Do What We Do in Life and Business* (2012), Ch. 1.

158. Ibid., p. 92.

159. Ibid., Ch. 3.

160. Will Durant, *The Story of Philosophy* (1961), p. 76.

161. The term used in Sanskrit is *ajnana* or *avidya*.

162. Ludwig Wittgenstein makes a similar observation. See Ludwig Wittgenstein, *Philosophical Occasions* (1993), p. 161.

CHAPTER 11

The Universal Teacher

U SUALLY OUR FRIENDS will not tell us what they really think of us. This is mainly because they know we don't want to hear it. If they give us honest feedback, we are liable to become angry, resentful or aggrieved. French philosopher and essayist Michel de Montaigne put it well:

> We need very strong ears to hear ourselves judged frankly;
> and because there are few who can endure frank criticism
> without being stung by it, those who venture to criticize us
> perform a remarkable act of friendship; for to undertake
> to wound and offend a man for his own good is to have a
> healthy love for him.[163]

We are living out a story, which we reinforce by repeating to others. We expect our friends to side with us. We want them to believe our story. A true friend, however, will remain kind but truthful with us, always.

The Dharma kings of the past were very careful to choose friends and advisers who would not flatter them or simply tell them what they wanted to hear. They therefore sought the company of enlightened Rishis and learned from them. These sages, having conquered the mind and senses, were free from the demands of the ego. Their allegiance to Truth was therefore unyielding; and they spoke with unearthly fearlessness, like the Rishis who addressed Alexander the Great.

There are many different categories and levels of advisers – from a caring teacher at school who sets us in the direction of our purpose to a dear friend who speaks to us with candour, to a wise Rishi of the highest level, the kind that once mentored kings and queens. According to the esoteric teachings of India, all teachers in our life are actually expressions of the same archetype, the "Universal Teacher", a manifestation of Vishnu seated within each of us.[164] The Universal Teacher assumes different forms in our life to lead us towards the fulfilment of our highest potential. If we are not aware or open, we will fail to honour the Universal Teacher in our life.

⚡ THE FIRST MANIFESTATION – THE INNER GUIDE ⚡

The Universal Teacher manifests before us in three different ways. The first is as our inner guide, the voice of Truth directing us from within.[165]

According to the Rishis, the Universal Teacher exists, first and foremost, within our heart. The people of primal India developed a great respect and sensitivity for this inner voice. We are able to grasp Dharma intuitively, not by the intellect but by a much deeper and more ancient faculty. Whenever we have what we sometimes call a "light-bulb moment", a moment of awakening to a deeper way of seeing, it is because we have heard and recognized the voice of Truth. We have the innate ability to recognize Truth, just as we know we are awake when we are awake. When we develop this faculty, we are able to hear the Universal Teacher speaking to us from within.

Hearing our own inner guide is not always easy, though. Our mind often speaks so loudly that we can no longer hear the voice of Truth. To hear this voice requires an inner stillness and a special kind of listening, known in India as "surrendered listening". This is when we listen with an open heart, and with a genuine desire to honour Truth in whatever way it reveals itself to us.

⚡ THE SECOND MANIFESTATION – THE MENTOR ⚡

Imagine we have an extraordinary natural gift – say, we were born to play the violin. Our talent will at first be raw and undeveloped. We can begin developing our skills by practising the violin on our own, but nothing will bring out our potential more fully and effectively as training under a master violinist. Our music teacher at school will be able to set us off in the right direction, but she will only be able to take us so far. But imagine if we were given the chance to train under Itzhak Perlman, or someone of his level. We would soon develop incredible tone, flawless technique, and a unique "presence" as a violinist. Our latent potential would emerge and blossom fully.

We may not all be natural musicians, but each of us was most definitely born on this earth to fulfil a particular purpose. Whether that purpose is "big" or "small", it is inexpressibly beautiful and deeply fulfilling for us. All purposes are actually very tiny, when looked at from the perspective of endless time and space. But when expressed perfectly, our purpose has breathtaking beauty, like the blossoming of a flower in the wilderness or the emergence of a navigational star on a dark, lonely road. We each have a unique potential to make a contribution of special worth in the world.

To better be able to reach us, the Universal Teacher sometimes manifests in our life as a caring, benevolent mentor. This can take the form of a parent, teacher or advisor who helps us on the path of Dharma. In India, such a person is traditionally regarded as a "guru", or mentor. Such a person will always place the interests of the student before his or her own. Importantly, a guru can help a student only as far as the level he or she is at herself. Thus, gurus are of many types with different capacities. The texts of India advise that we try to learn from a guru of the highest level.[166]

These texts actually set out very clearly the qualifications of such a guru. These qualities are remarkable, and have for thousands of years been considered a prerequisite to teaching the sacred lore of the Rishis. They are the benchmark against which any mentor should be measured, and the standard to which all genuine mentors will aspire.

The *Skanda Purana* explains that the syllable *gu* stands for "darkness" and *ru* for "illumination". A true guru is therefore someone who dispels the darkness of illusion with the light of transformative wisdom.[167] A genuine guru will have deep knowledge of the ancient texts. That knowledge will be realized knowledge and not merely intellectual learning.[168] In other words, it will be perfectly reflected in the way he or she lives. Thus, a true guru will embody Truth, Purity, Non-violence and Discipline in his life. Just to make sure there is no mistake about it, I am not such a teacher, although I have had the great privilege in my life to meet one. I struggle to live by the Dharma principles on most days. But my ardent hope is one day to become a perfect student.

The teachings of India were for thousands of years passed down from master to student in an oral tradition, long before they were ever written down.[169] One of the best-known examples of the relationship between guru and disciple is to be found in the *Bhagavad-gita*, in the battlefield conversation between Krishna and Arjuna.

While academic study of ancient texts may provide us with some information, it will generally not yield transformation. It has no power to alter the way we perceive the world. In the *Mahabharata*, Yudhisthira therefore explains that the mere study of texts will not yield true knowledge of Dharma because such knowledge is concealed not in texts, but in the hearts of the great masters who embody it.[170] By learning directly from such a master, we can become living embodiments of Dharma ourselves.

Importantly, an ideal guru has complete mastery over their mind and senses. That means they have conquered the six urges – the impetus to speak, the agitation of the mind, the onset of anger, the vehemence of the tongue, the urge of the belly, and the agitation of lust.[171] Thus, they will not be driven by a desire for money, fame or followers. In the *Skanda Purana*, Mahadeva warns pointedly:

> Numerous are the gurus who rob their disciples of their wealth. But I consider it rare to find a guru who instead steals away the miseries from the disciple's heart.[172]

Another text similarly explains:

> One who desires to obtain wealth, fame or service from his students is not fit to become a guru. A true guru is an ocean of compassion, is fulfilled within himself, and works tirelessly for the benefit of others.[173]

The sacred texts advise that a prospective guru and disciple should examine each other carefully for at least one full year before formalizing a guru-disciple relationship.[174] In this way they will come to know each other's real nature. This is the best way to understand whether a guru is qualified.

⁕ THE THIRD MANIFESTATION – THE ENVIRONMENT ⁕

Our environment is overflowing with wisdom too. There are teachers all around us to help us, if we care to look. They are all manifestations of the Universal Teacher. For instance, water teaches us fluidity and adaptability. The past teaches us humility and the extent of our own folly in life. Stillness and silence teach us clarity. Young children teach us honesty and authenticity. Our teachers are everywhere. They speak to us through all things. We hear their wisdom in our heart. The Universal Teacher, who resides within us, manifests in these different external forms to better reach us.

Suffering is an important teacher too. Many people spend their whole life running away from it. But suffering deepens us, and teaches us compassion and empathy. It also teaches us detachment.[175] Most human beings go through at least one period in their life marked by intense difficulty and pain. If they look back to that time, they often acknowledge also that it was the period in which they learned the most about life. When we experience intense suffering, at some point we cast aside the causes of our suffering and experience immense inner freedom. When this happens, we advance far on the path of Dharma.

Even anger, irritation and disgust are teachers. If we see something that irritates or unnerves us, we can look deeply. It always tells us something about ourselves. Indeed, our so-called enemies can be our greatest teachers. Baltasar Gracián observed, "A wise man gets more use from his enemies than a fool from his friends."[176]

It took me many years even to begin appreciating that my environment might actually be helping me at all times. So I might understand, my teacher one day told me about a powerful king named Yadu, who met a young and effulgent brahmin while travelling through his kingdom.

The king approached the brahmin and said, "Dear brahmin, although all people within this world are burning in the great forest fire of desire and greed, I see that you remain free and are not burned by that fire. You are just like a mighty elephant who takes refuge from a blazing forest fire by standing in the cooling waters of the Ganges. Please tell me how you became enlightened, so I may learn from you."[177]

The brahmin replied, "I have learned from twenty-four different gurus. They include the earth, wind, ocean, honey thief, hawk and arrow maker. By taking their lessons to heart, I have attained complete freedom from suffering."

The brahmin then explained to King Yadu what he had learned from each of his teachers. "I observed that the earth provides for everyone's needs," he said, "even when humans plunder her resources, turn her lush forests into wasteland, and soak her surface with blood in the most savage of wars. From the earth I therefore learned the quality of tolerance. Similarly, the trees of the earth give their bark, roots, fruits, leaves, wood and shade, without any expectation of return. This taught me the quality of dedication to others. It taught me to make the welfare of others the sole reason for my existence."[178]

The brahmin continued: "The wind travels everywhere, sometimes passing through a waterfall, a fragrant sandalwood forest or a crematorium. The wind crosses through dark and forbidding places, yet remains unafraid. It carries the aromas of different locations, but remains unentangled and undisturbed. From the wind, I therefore learned that while we may find ourselves in challenging and troublesome situations in life, we can remain fearless and undisturbed, thereby transcending 'good' and 'bad'.[179]

"From the ocean, I learned that whatever life brings our way, we should remain undiminished in who we are. During the rainy season, the rivers rushing to the sea are overflowing; and during the summer, they dry up. But the ocean always remains unmoved and inexhaustible. Similarly, a wise person is never shaken, even in the midst of the greatest difficulties. She remains at peace whether she meets with success or failure. This is because she does not seek her identity in these things. Therefore, they do not define her."[180]

The brahmin continued: "One day I happened to see a person in the forest breaking open a bee hive to collect all the honey that the countless bees had spent their entire lives producing. From this I learned about the dangers and futility of needless accumulation of capital, which simply creates greed, danger and fear. Humans can be like bees who struggle to produce a large quantity of honey, which is then stolen by a more powerful capitalist for his own enjoyment or benefit. If our wealth is not lost during our life, death will in the end surely take everything from us. Therefore, I concluded that I should not make the amassing of capital an end in its own right. Rather, the primary purpose of wealth is to help others.[181]

"One day, I observed a group of large hawks in flight. Unable to find any prey, the hawks suddenly combined together to attack a weaker hawk that was holding some meat. The weaker hawk dodged this way and that, to save itself. At last, the weaker hawk, its life in peril, gave up the meat it was holding on to, and at that moment it was freed from misery. Seeing this, I understood that humans form deep attachments to objects and outcomes, which they believe will make them happy. But these attachments are actually a source of suffering. As soon as we relinquish our possessiveness and attachment, we at once become liberated from suffering.[182]

"Another time, I observed an arrow maker at work. Suddenly drums, trumpets and other musical instruments could be heard, as a large procession approached. Despite all the commotion, the arrow maker was so absorbed in his work that he did not even see or notice the king, who passed right next to him. This filled me with wonder. Most of us, I thought, are continually distracted by the daily commotion of life. We are filled with thoughts about the past and dreams about the future, so that we are rarely fully present to what we are doing. If we could live with presence, how our life would be transformed.[183]

"In this way, I learned from twenty-four different teachers. I took their teachings to heart and began applying them in my own life. This is how I attained enlightenment."

Hearing this, King Yadu accepted this effulgent and fearless brahmin as his guru. The king developed the same qualities as the brahmin, and began ruling his vast kingdom as a philosopher-king.

⸗ THE ENVIRONMENT IS ALWAYS FRIENDLY ⸗

Unfortunately, the ability to recognize intuitive wisdom seems to be a capacity we have largely bred out of ourselves, as humans. We have been preoccupied predominantly with developing the analytical and intellectual capabilities of the mind, leaving what we might call the "intuitive mind" to wither.

If we are awake to the voice of Truth, if we hear that voice speaking to us through all things, we realize that the environment is always friendly. It is not hostile. There is actually beauty and perfection in all things. For a person committed to the path of Dharma, her perceptual universe is always helpful. Such a person perceives opportunity all about her, even in times of difficulty. As William Shakespeare eloquently put it: "Sweet are the uses of adversity, Which like the toad, ugly and venomous, Wears yet a precious jewel in his head."[184]

Everything within the environment is actually helping us on our journey to wisdom; everything is sympathetic to us from all sides. It takes a special awareness to actually perceive this.

In every challenge or difficulty there lies hidden a jewel for us to find and keep. Most of us see only the outer form of the circumstance and never look for that hidden jewel. We are simply unable to see it because it lies in a direction we don't often look – within. The things that are hardest to find or reach are not those that are furthest from us, but those that are closest to us. It requires inward-looking perception to recognize the opportunities for inner freedom and growth that exist even in the challenges in our life.

Life's most important lessons require that we, ourselves, set out on an inner journey. There is no shortcut. As Marcel Proust wrote:

> We do not receive wisdom, we must discover it for ourselves, after a journey through the wilderness which no one else can make for us, which no one can spare us, for our wisdom is the point of view from which we come at last to regard the world.[185]

Like all journeys worth taking, we may at times be uncomfortable or exposed. We may have to look into the abyss of the unknown. The point of maximum confusion is often the point of maximum learning.

Every step forward requires that we release a current foothold. We cannot move forward if we refuse to progress from where we are right now. Thus, anyone who insists on comfort, safety and security as primary conditions of life will be incapable of developing wisdom.

Notes

163. Michel de Montaigne, "Of Experience" (1587–88); in Michel de Montaigne, *The Complete Essays of Montaigne* (1973), p. 825.

164. *Bhagavata Purana*, 11.29.6, as well as Shrila Krishnadasa Kaviraja Goswami, *Shri Chaitanya-charitamrita*, Adi-lila, 1.47 and 1.58, and Madhya, 22.47. In the esoteric Bhakti tradition, the Universal Teacher is worshipped as Paramatma or Vishnu, the all-pervading sustainer of all things and the protector of Dharma. One of the 1008 names of Vishnu is Guru, or "Teacher".

165. In ancient India, the inner guide is known as Paramatma. For key references to Paramatma, see *Mundaka Upanishad*, 3.1.2; *Shvetashvatara Upanishad*, 4.7; *Bhagavad-gita*, 6.7 and 15.15; and *Bhagavata Purana*, 1.2.11.

166. *Skanda Purana*, "The Song of the Teacher" (*Guru-gita*), 279–81. A topmost guru is known as *parama-guru* or *sad-guru*.

167. *Skanda Purana*, 44.

168. See *Bhagavata Purana*, 11.3.21; *Mundaka Upanishad*, 1.2.12; and Shri Sanatana Goswami, *Shri Hari-bhakti-vilasa*, 1.46. See also *Bhagavad-gita*, 4.34, in which Krishna describes the genuine guru as *tattva-darshinah*, a "seer of Truth".

169. Indeed, the Sanskrit term *upanishad* itself is often said to derive from the Sanskrit words *upa* ("near"), *ni* ("down") and *shad* ("to sit"), meaning "to sit down near" a guru to receive instruction.

170. *Mahabharata*, Vana-parva, 313.117.

171. Shri Rupa Goswami, *Shri Upadeshamrita*, 1.

172. *Skanda Purana*, "The Song of the Teacher" (*Guru-gita*), 269.

173. *Vishnu-smriti*; quoted by Shri Sanatana Goswami in his *Shri Hari-bhakti-vilasa*, 1.45.

174. Shri Sanatana Goswami, *Shri Hari-bhakti-vilasa*, 1.73–76. Shri Sanatana Goswami quotes verses from *Mantra-muktavali* and *Sara-sangraha*.

175. *Bhagavata Purana*, 11.8.38 and 11.9.1.

176. Baltasar Gracián, *Art of Worldly Wisdom* (2003), p. 49.

177. *Bhagavata Purana*, 11.7.29.

178. *Bhagavata Purana,* 11.7.37–38.

179. *Bhagavata Purana,* 11.7.40–41.

180. *Bhagavata Purana,* 11.8.5–6. See also *Bhagavad-gita,* 2.70.

181. *Bhagavata Purana,* 11.8.15. On death, see *Bhagavad-gita,* 10.34.

182. *Bhagavata Purana,* 11.9.1–2.

183. *Bhagavata Purana,* 11.9.13.

184. William Shakespeare, *As You Like It,* Act 2, Scene 1.

185. Marcel Proust, *In Search of Lost Time,* Vol. 2, *Within a Budding Grove* (1992), p. 513.

CHAPTER 12

The Esoteric Secrets
of the Dharma Code

H IS BODY WAS BLOATED AND UNMOVING. We placed him on a stretcher and carried him in a small procession to Shamshan Ghat at the far end of Mathura, where the dead are burned and their ashes dispersed into the Yamuna river. It was past sunset and by the time we arrived, the only source of light was the blazing fires of the dead. There were four, each at a different stage of conflagration.

We brought firewood and began to stack it. The head of the monastery rubbed ghee, or clarified butter, in large handfuls over the dead monk. Soon the firewood was stacked so high that only the monk's feet were visible. The funeral pyre was set ablaze to the recitation of mantras from the Vedas. Flames burst six feet into the air. The smell was difficult to bear, like the odour of burning hair.

There were strange mendicants who lived in the crematorium. Smeared with ashes, they had reddish eyes. When they walked, they moved this way and that, as if possessed by a hoard of ghosts. I made my way to the river, giving them a wide berth. In the dark waters of the river were a hundred lights, still and unblinking. These were the eyes of river turtles. Poor families could not always afford as much firewood as they needed to burn their dead. Whatever was left among the ashes was scooped up and cast into the river, a moment these scavengers had learned to anticipate eagerly.

Life is fragile and ephemeral. It passes us by in the blink of an eye. A haunting verse from a compendium of Dharma teachings came to mind:

> Wealth is temporary, like specks of dust on the feet. Youth flows away as swiftly as a mountain river. Life is like a quivering bead of water on a lily leaf. This body is transitory like foam. Therefore, one who does not open the gates of heaven by deeds of Dharma will be overtaken by old age and remorse and thus burn in the fire of lamentation.[186]

The "gates of heaven" are the extraordinary deeds we are capable of that bring out our god-like qualities, our higher self.

I recalled my own close encounters with death. When I was eight, I didn't know yet how to swim and was afraid of deep water. But when someone tried to throw a large block of clay at me, I jumped into a river and was swept downstream into a whirlpool, and very nearly drowned.

I remembered also how by the same river I was at now, the Yamuna, a friend had been robbed by bandits a few years earlier. He had tried to fight them off. One of them had then pulled out a home-made pipe-gun and shot him in the abdomen. The twenty-three pieces of metal shrapnel had inexplicably missed his vital organs and he had survived. I remember hearing the shot and seeing the blood. We forget how short and precious life is, and most of us waste it away in conforming to expectations and leading a very small, self-centred life.

I remembered reading about how Yudhisthira had been challenged by a Yaksha, the guardian of a forest lake who had caused Yudhisthira's four brothers to fall to the ground in a death-like stupor. If Yudhisthira answered the Yaksha's questions correctly, his brothers would live. The Yaksha had asked, "What is Dharma about in a single word?"

"Skill," Yudhisthira had replied. Put differently, Dharma is about living with great skill.

"What is the greatest wonder in this world?" the Yaksha had asked.

Yudhisthira had replied: "Day after day, countless living entities make their way to death; but those that remain behave as if they will live forever. What can be more wonderful than this?"

In the course of living, we forget about Dharma and about our purpose in life. We are covered by a veil of illusion and impurity.[187]

⁂ THE FURNACE OF PURIFICATION ⁂

When I was much younger, following my morning meditation, I could sometimes observe the covering of illusion over people, like a subtle haze that enveloped them.

As I watched people walk down the street, immersed in their life, I could see that some had a very pronounced, thick and dark fog around them, while others were enfolded by a lighter miasma. I understood that it depended upon the level of Purity in their life. But after thirty minutes or so I would lose myself again in that same haze, so that I could no longer distinguish or discern it.

Once, I experienced the force of my consciousness, the soul, rise above my body to the top of my head. In that moment I could see the world with breathtaking clarity and an aching compassion. I could understand why the Rishis had chosen just the words they did in the sacred texts. What they were describing was actually difficult to put in words; but if it were to be expressed, those were the perfect words to render it. Then, despite my longing to remain in that joyful state free from suffering, I felt my consciousness slip back into the thick coverings of illusion of my mind and physical body. I was once again in the grip of my small, worldly perspective in life, the stranglehold of my ego and false sense of identity in the world.

Ultimately, the purpose of the Dharma Code is to help us become an enlightened Rishi ourselves, free from illusion. The horizontal axis of the Dharma Code, or the axis of Discipline and Purity, is the "furnace of purification". The vertical axis of the Dharma Code, or the axis of Truth and Non-violence, is the "ladder from exploitation to dedication". In my own tradition, it is the pursuit of Bhakti, or selfless love. As the great sage Narada says, "Bhakti is the dearest possession of one who adheres to Truth by body, mind and words."[188]

It is through a process of purification that we are able to see things as they are and become what we are meant to be. The furnace of purification is the alchemical fire that transforms us into a philosopher-king or queen. It does this through smelting, a process by which pure metal is extracted from its ore. One great teacher in our tradition has explained it as follows:

> The gold should be cast into the fire. When the alloy portion vanishes [is burned off] then the real gold will be visible. Now the pure gold is mixed with some alloy. So "Die to Live" – throw yourself into the fire.[189]

There is greatness, or pure gold, within each of us; but it needs to be extracted. We cannot become what we are capable of if we cling so tightly to what we are right now. The Rishis, who were masters of potentiality, recognized our divine nature. The Dharma Code is an alchemical system for awakening to our true spiritual consciousness. It is an ancient technology that ultimately leads us to break down the illusions in our life, starting with our false sense of self. It allows us to see that we exist beyond the play of form of this temporary world.

When we look for ourselves in our field of perception, it is like searching a movie for a view of the camera man. Whatever is visible in the field of perception is not who we are. This is why it is sometimes said we are not material but spiritual beings. Nobel physicist Erwin Schrödinger makes this point succinctly:

So, in brief, we do not belong to this material world that science constructs for us. We are not in it, we are outside. We are only spectators. The reason why we believe that we are in it, that we belong to the picture, is that our bodies are in the picture. Our bodies belong to it.[190]

Our physical body is part of the content of perception. It changes continually over time. Most cells in the body are replaced over a period of seven years. That means our body of seven years ago has been ecologically dispersed throughout the environment. We are not fat, thin, young or old. These attributes relate only to the body.

We are also not the lead character in the story of our life. That lead character is simply a figment of our imagination. Our involvement in this world is much like that of a person caught up in a dream, or to use a more contemporary analogy, a person trapped in a virtual world. It creates an "optical delusion of consciousness", to borrow an expression from Albert Einstein.[191] That optical delusion imprisons us.

We are not material beings who have spiritual experiences: we are spiritual beings who have lost ourselves in a material experience. When we discover this, not as an idea but as a deep perceptual awareness, then we are released from suffering. Even a slight recognition of our spiritual nature brings enormous peace and strength into our life.

⚘ THE ASCENT FROM EXPLOITATION TO LOVE ⚘

During a pilgrimage in India, I arrived at the ancient forest known as Madhuvana. I climbed the hill that led to the temple of Vishnu, the maintainer of Dharma, and of Narada, the great Rishi. It is said that Vishnu has four arms and carries a fiery disc-like weapon, a conch, a lotus and a club. He is the colour of a monsoon rain cloud and more brilliant than lightning. The ancient mystical texts say he cannot be seen with the material eye or understood with the material mind.[192] His very form is made of love and affection, and therefore he remains invisible to the heart hardened by violence and devoid of love.

Ancient legend has it that a young prince who had been rejected by his father had come to this desolate forest, filled with bitterness. Here he had meditated on Vishnu, who had fulfilled his wish to have a kingdom even greater than that of his father. But in satisfying this wish, Vishnu had also purified the boy of bitterness, ego and the thirst of worldly want, transforming him into a great Dharma king.

When I was young, I used to catch dandelion seeds in the wind during school breaks because I had heard you could make a wish on them. But what is truly worth wishing for? The texts of India speak of the "seed of desire".[193] An entire future is contained within the tiniest of seeds. Our desires are like seeds. They have an invisible organizing power in our perceptual world. I knew, even as a young boy, that I should be careful what I desire. Holding the dandelion seeds in my hand, I would wish for Bhakti, which I knew was very precious, even if I didn't quite understand what it was. I would then release the seeds into the wind and watch them rise into the air, wishing them a safe voyage to wherever they were meant to go.

Some people make it their driving desire to accumulate capital; others to stand out through achievement; others to exert power or control; and others to find pleasure through fine food or sexual conquest. People will spend a full lifetime pursuing a purpose like this, but in the end will feel a sadness or emptiness in their life. They will feel they have somehow missed the mark. Their achievements or wealth may sparkle in the eyes of others who pursue the same trajectory, but in their old age they may feel an ordinariness about their life. This is because the trajectory they took was ordinary.

I now wanted to know more about Bhakti, the trajectory I had wished for so many times. Thinking about it, I realized I had never been a very loving person. All my life I had been so absorbed in my own small story that I had been largely oblivious to the suffering of others. I wondered how in my own tradition, the Bhakti tradition, one might progress from a life of want and exploitation to a life of dedication, free from violence.

I had come to Madhuvana with many other pilgrims, headed by my teacher. As if reading my mind, my teacher began telling us about Narada Rishi, who had advised the young boy Dhruva to fix his mind on Vishnu, the personification of Dharma. Later, my teacher told us another story about Narada, one that helped me better understand the ladder from violence to selfless love.

One day, Narada Rishi was making his way to where three rivers – the Ganges, Yamuna and Saraswati – meet. On the forest path he saw a deer pierced by an arrow. The creature's legs were broken, and it was twitching in pain, leaving a trail of blood. A little further down the path, Narada saw a boar in the same state, and then a rabbit. The sage was pained to see the agony of these creatures.

Further on, Narada spotted a hunter concealed behind a tree, his reddish eyes gleaming in the shadows. Arrows in hand, the hunter was preparing himself to kill another creature.

Narada left the forest path and approached the hunter. As he did so the animals in the woods scattered. The hunter, his plans foiled, turned to the sage to rebuke him. But the great sage's effulgent presence seemed to prevent the hunter from being able to speak harshly. Instead, the hunter began by respectfully introducing himself as Mrigari. He asked Narada why he had strayed from the forest path.

"I have come to ask you why you leave your animals half-dead," Narada replied gently. "Why don't you kill them completely?"

"My father taught me to kill animals this way," Mrigari said. "In fact, I quite like to see them twitching in pain. It gives me no end of pleasure."

"I have a favour to beg of you," Narada said.

"Sure. If you want any of these animals, you can take them. If you like, I also have plenty of skins – deer and even tiger skins."

"No, I don't need any skins," said the sage. "I ask only that from this day on you kill your animals completely, and don't leave them half-dead."

The hunter seemed bewildered. "Why are you asking me that? They are just animals. What difference does it make how I kill them?"

Narada had to explain. "You are intentionally causing these creatures immense pain. What goes around comes around. By the law of karma, you will have to experience great pain in your life too. As a hunter, you make your living by killing. This is a slight *aparadha*, or disrespect; but when you intentionally leave these creatures writhing in pain, your disrespect has no limit – and in the end, it will destroy you."

Usually, the hunter would have paid no heed to such words. But Narada was a self-realized sage, and his words had the potency to cut through the dense fog of the hunter's boorishness. Mrigari felt the truth of Narada's statements, and it made him uneasy. He now recalled the decades of unspeakable misery he had inflicted upon his defenceless victims. Suddenly, he remembered their tortured cries, their trembling, the futile pleading in their eyes – and for the first time in his life, he could feel their pain. This sudden awakening, which the sage had brought about, filled him with remorse and fear.

"I have caused great suffering," Mrigari admitted at last. His face seemed pained. His eyes were clear. The truth can sometimes be terrible to behold, and the hunter pleaded for help. "How can I undo this?" he asked.

Narada instructed the hunter first to break his bow. He assured him that by turning his back on violence, good fortune would enter his world. The universe itself would conspire to maintain him. Narada then instructed Mrigari in the teachings of Bhakti-yoga, the "yoga of devotion". In the Bhakti tradition, unconditional, selfless love is regarded as the highest stage of spiritual enlightenment. In this esoteric tradition, such selfless love is developed by directing it to Vishnu, the Supreme Origin, in whom all things rest; and as a result, that unconditional affection automatically spreads out like the rays of the sun to touch all living beings, without distinction or prejudice.[194] By devotion to Vishnu without ulterior motive or pretension, the Bhakti practitioner develops the counter-habit of loving and leaves no room for violence in her life. The *Bhagavad-gita* describes this yoga as the pinnacle and ultimate end of all forms of yoga.[195]

In its ultimate expression, the Dharma principle of Nonviolence is about living through deeds of love. This is the way to use our energy fully in the service of life. If we could wrap every thought we have in unconditional love, if we could express love in everything we say or do, our life would be utterly transformed.

Taking the hunter with him, Narada went to find the three animals that had been left half-dead. Narada stroked them gently, and by his potency revived them. The creatures got up and swiftly fled, leaving the hunter wide-eyed.

Months later, Narada Rishi decided to visit Mrigari, accompanied by a sage named Parvata Rishi. Mrigari, who now lived on the riverbank, seemed to shine with potency. Recognizing Narada, he ran to meet him, filled with excitement. But Mrigari began behaving strangely as he moved forward. He suddenly stooped forward and began fanning the ground. As Narada and Parvata Rishi approached, they saw that the former hunter was trying to whisk away ants on the ground with a cloth, ever so gently to avoid hurting them, so that he could prostrate himself before his teacher, as is the tradition in India.

Narada smiled to see the hunter's tenderness of heart. "By meditating on Vishnu, good qualities like compassion come naturally, as a side effect," Narada explained. "Such a person cannot tolerate the pain of any living being."

In a short time, Mrigari had attained the advanced stages of Bhakti-yoga. Tears of affection now welled up in his eyes to see his teacher. By following the instructions of an enlightened sage, Mrigari had mastered the principle of Non-violence. He had developed the counter-habit of Bhakti, or unconditional love, and had perfected all four dimensions of Dharma.[196]

Hearing this account from my teacher awakened a strong desire in me to progress on the path of Bhakti.

⚹ A STRANGE DREAM ⚹

On Friday, 2 November 2012, I dreamed of a large, powerful bull as white and as soft as milk. The bull looked at me, and without so much as moving his mouth, began to speak. He said he was the embodiment of Dharma, a manifestation of Vishnu in this world. He explained that Vishnu maintains the four Dharma principles with his four mighty arms. The bull then said that all the answers I sought were contained in the *Bhagavata Purana*, the same text that sets out the Dharma Code.

At this point, I woke up. Usually, I don't remember my dreams; but this one had been especially vivid and deeply instructive. I checked the time. It was 3:00am.

I am not a great believer in dreams. They can so easily be simply the imaginative creation of an overactive mind. I tried to put my dream aside; but something kept drawing me to it. In the end, I found myself searching through the thousands of verses of the *Bhagavata Purana*. What I found set my heart racing with delight.

Not only does the ancient text depict Dharma as a white bull, whose four legs are Truth, Purity, Non-violence and Discipline, but it also explains clearly that Vishnu manifests as this bull. The ancient text states that those who apply the principles of Dharma in their everyday life please Vishnu.[197]

I also learned that Vishnu's effulgent discus, known as Sudarshan, grants perception of the highest Truth. Sudarshan means "auspicious vision". Vishnu's conch represents Purity. Always filled with the breath of Vishnu, it makes sounds like a thunder cloud, dispersing those who are averse to Dharma and filling those dedicated to Dharma with joy. Vishnu's lotus represents the good fortune of Bhakti, or selfless love free from violence. Vishnu's club represents Discipline. It smashes the fiendish obstacles that prevent us from perfecting our life wholeheartedly. Yogis meditate on this forceful club, which is very dear to Vishnu and which is a manifestation of the Universal Teacher.[198]

We are each a minute fragment of Vishnu, the resting place of all beings. Therefore by developing unconditional love for Vishnu, we automatically develop unconditional love and affection for all beings. The *Bhagavata Purana* explains that one who makes his entire life an uninterrupted work of love without self-interest practises the highest form of Dharma and achieves complete fulfilment.[199] This, the *Bhagavad-gita* also reveals, is the true "secret of kings, guarded by kings".[200]

⚞ THE ARCHAEOLOGY OF THE SELF ⚟

We all experience basic needs, such as hunger, thirst and fatigue. We are conditioned to satisfy these needs by *getting* something – food, drink or rest. Mistakenly, we conclude that by getting, we can achieve fulfilment also. We think that by acquiring things we can have a fully filled, or "fulfilled", life. Feeling empty and dissatisfied, we are constantly filling up on consumer goods and services, forever consuming and swallowing. But we never quite feel satiated.

This is because we are placing things above people, matter above life. Things cannot quench the thirst of the soul. People are meant to be loved; and things are meant to be used. But we become so confused that we love things and use people. When we adopt this approach, we get caught up in a web of violence and exploitation. But when we adopt a life-orientated approach, one that privileges the highest principle of Dharma, we begin to ascend the ladder of dedication, the pathway to awakening our capacity to love unconditionally. The Rishis explain that this is the true, authentic nature of the soul.

Happiness is our natural state of being when the edifice of illusion is removed or stripped away.[201] Therefore, the way to happiness is not to try to create it. Rather, it is to seek everything that *obstructs* it. There is no need to try to *become* happy. It's sufficient simply to remove what blocks or obstructs our inborn happiness.

Thus, happiness is "excavated". It is brought out of ourselves, like the cleaning of a dusty mirror or the shining of a brilliant gemstone. When we look inward and invoke Dharma in our life, our true nature and beauty immediately begin to shine through. By applying Truth, Purity, Non-violence and Discipline in our everyday life, we manifest our concealed potential.

When we seek happiness, what we are actually yearning for is the full awakening of our own true nature, the sacred self free from imprisonment in illusion. We are a priceless gem concealed deep within strata of illusion, conditioning and bewilderment. The archaeology of wisdom is therefore the excavation of the self. That process of discovering ourselves is what the path of Dharma is about.

The Dharma Code helps us engage with life in a particular way, one that generates vitality and manifests our highest potential. It is an ancient technology for creating "vital engagement", by helping us make enlightened choices in our everyday life. Guided by the Dharma Code, we are able to fulfil our primary duty in life, our duty of happiness.

Notes

186. *Hitopadesha*, 1.148. This rendition is based on the translation from Satya Narayana Dasa, *The Hitopadesa of Sri Narayana Pandita*, Book One (1997), pp. 214–5.

187. See *Mahabharata*, 3.295–99.

188. *Shri Narada-bhakti-sutra*, 81.

189. Shrila B. R. Shridhara Maharaja, "The Panacea", *Rays of The Harmonist*, No.11 (Karttika, 2002), p. 22.

190. Erwin Schrödinger, *Nature and the Greeks* (1954), p. 94.

191. Albert Einstein, letter of 1950, as quoted in *The New York Times* (29 March 1972) and *The New York Post* (28 November 1972).

192. For example, the *Shvetashvatara Upanishad* (4.20), which belongs to the *Yajur Veda*, states, "His form is beyond material sense perception. No one can see him with material eyes." See also the *Kena Upanishad* (1.3–8), which belongs to the *Sama Veda*. Vishnu is referred to as Adhokshaja because he is beyond the purview of the material senses and mind.

193. *Bija-anushayah*, "the seed of desire". For instance, see *Bhagavata Purana*, 7.7.36 and 12.6.68.

194. For example, see *Bhagavata Purana*, 3.25.21 and 4.31.14. See also *Bhagavad-gita*, 10.8.

195. *Bhagavad-gita*, 6.47.

196. Adapted from the *Skanda Purana*, as retold by Shri Krishnadas Kaviraja Goswami in *Shri Chaitanya-charitamrita* (Madhya, 24.230–282).

197. Dharma in the form of a white bull: *Bhagavata Purana*, 1.17.22. The bull's four legs are the four Dharma principles: *Bhagavata Purana*, 1.17.24. Vishnu manifests as the bull of Dharma: *Bhagavata Purana*, 11.17.11. By applying these Dharma principles, a person is able to please Vishnu: e.g. *Bhagavata Purana*, 7.11.8–12; see also *Shri Narada Bhakti Sutra*, 78.

198. Vishnu's discus, known as Sudarshana Chakra: *Bhagavata Purana*, 9.5.3–7. Vishnu's conch, known as Panchajanya: *Bhagavata Purana*, 6.8.25 and 10.59.6. Vishnu's lotus: an emblem in the hand of the Goddess of Fortune (e.g. *Bhagavata Purana*, 4.20.27) that represents auspiciousness, especially the auspiciousness of Bhakti to Vishnu, whose feet are compared to lotus flowers (e.g. *Bhagavata Purana*, 4.9.12). Vishnu's club, known as Kaumodaki: *Bhagavata Purana*, 3.28.28 and 6.8.24.

199. *Bhagavata Purana*, 1.2.6.

200. *Bhagavad-gita*, 9.2.

201. See *Bhagavad-gita*, 18.54. The nature of the self when free from illusion is *prasanna-atma*, "fully joyful".

Bibliography

ALLEN, JAMES, *The Life Triumphant: Mastering the Heart and Mind* (New York: Cosimo, 2007).

AL-NAWAWI, IMAM YAHYA, *Al-Nawawi Forty Hadiths and Commentary*, trans. Arabic Virtual Translation Center (New York: Arabic Virtual Translation Center, 2010).

ARISTOTLE, *Nichomachean Ethics*, trans. M. Ostwald (Indianapolis, Indiana: Bobbs-Merrill, 1962).

ARRIAN, *The Campaigns of Alexander*, trans. Aubrey de Sélincourt (London: Penguin Books, 1971).

BAUER, ELVIRA, *Trau keinem Fuchs auf grüner Heid und keinem Jud auf seinem Eid* [trans. Trust No Fox on his Green Heath and No Jew on his Oath] (Nuremberg: Stürmer Verlag, 1936). <http://www.calvin.edu/academic/cas/gpa/fuchs.htm>. Accessed 13 November 2011.

BAUMEISTER, ROY F., JENNIFER D. CAMPBELL, JOACHIM I. KRUEGER and KATHLEEN D. VOHS, "Exploding the Self-esteem Myth", *Scientific American Mind*, Vol. 16, No. 4 (December 2005), pp. 50–57.

BAUMEISTER, ROY F., and JOHN TIERNEY, *Willpower: Rediscovering Our Greatest Strength* (London: Allen Lane, 2012).

BEZOS, JEFF, Princeton University graduation address
(May 2010). <http://www.ted.com/talks/jeff_
bezos_gifts_vs_choices.html>. Accessed 30 July
2010.

BHAKTIVEDANTA SWAMI PRABHUPADA, A. C.,
Bhagavad-gita As It Is (New York: Macmillan,1972).

—— *Shri Caitanya-caritamrita* (BhaktivedantaVedaBase
2003, Bhaktivedanta Archives, Bhaktivedanta Book
Trust).

—— *Shri Ishopanishad* (Bhaktivedanta VedaBase 2003,
Bhaktivedanta Archives, Bhaktivedanta Book Trust).

—— *Shrimad-Bhagavatam* (Bhaktivedanta VedaBase 2003,
Bhaktivedanta Archives, Bhaktivedanta Book Trust).

—— *Shri Narada-bhakti-sutra* (Bhaktivedanta VedaBase
2003, Bhaktivedanta Archives, Bhaktivedanta Book
Trust).

BHAKTIVINODA THAKURA, SHRILA, *Jaiva-dharma*,
trans. Shri Shrimad Bhaktivedanta Narayana
Maharaja (Mathura: Gaudiya Vedanta Prakashan,
2008).

BRILLAT-SAVARIN, JEAN ANTHELME, *Physiologie du Goût*
(1848), ed. Gabriel de Gonet (published as an
e-book by Project Gutenberg, 23 Sep. 2007),
Aphorisme IV. <http://www gutenberg.org/files/
22741/22741-h/22741-h.htm>.
Accessed 29 Dec. 2007.

BÜHLER, GEORG, trans., *The Laws of Manu*
(New York: Dover, 1969).

BYROM, THOMAS, *Dhammapada: The Sayings of the Buddha*

(Boston and London: Shambhala
Publications, 1993).

CHEVALIER, SOPHIE, and ANNE MONJARET,
"Getting Gifting", *Scientific American Mind*,
Vol. 16, No. 4 (December 2005), pp.12–13.

CHOMSKY, NOAM, *Knowledge of Language: Its Nature,
Origin, and Use* (Westport, Connecticut:
Greenwood Publishing Group, 1986).

CHURCHILL, WINSTON, speech in the House of Commons,
17 May 1916. <http://hansardmillbanksystems.com/
commons/1916/may/17/royal-assent#column
_1578>. Accessed 12 March 2012.

COVEY, STEPHEN R., *The 8th Habit: From Effectiveness
to Greatness* (New York: Free Press, 2005).

DASA, SATYA NARAYANA, *The Hitopadesa of Sri Narayana
Pandita, Book One* (Faridabad, India: Jiva Institute,
1997).

DE GRAAF, JOHN, DAVID WANN and THOMAS H. NAYLOR,
Affluenza: The All-Consuming Epidemic (San
Francisco: Berrett-Koehler Publishers, 2001).

DE MONTAIGNE, MICHEL, *The Complete Essays of Montaigne*,
trans. Donald M. Frame (Stanford, California:
Stanford University Press, 1973).

DHARMATRATA (compiler), *Udanavarga*, ed. Franz
Bernhard (Göttingen: Vandenhoek & Ruprecht,
1965); published on Ancient Buddhist Texts
[website]. <http://www.ancient-buddhist-texts.net/
Buddhist-Texts/S1-Udanavarga/index.htm>.
Published January 2005 (version 2.1). Accessed 29
November 2012.

DUHIGG, CHARLES, *The Power of Habit: Why We Do What We Do in Life and Business* (New York: Random House, 2012).

DURANT, WILL, *The Story of Philosophy: The Lives and Opinions of the World's Greatest Philosophers from Plato to John Dewey* (New York: Pocket Books, 1961).

EDGERTON, FRANKLIN (trans. and ed.), *Vikrama's Adventures or The Thirty-two Tales of the Throne* [*Vikrama-charita*], Volumes 26–27 of the Harvard Oriental Series (Harvard University Press, 1926).

EINSTEIN, ALBERT, letter of 1950, as quoted in *The New York Times* (29 March 1972) and *The New York Post* (28 November 1972).

ELLIS, ALBERT, *Feeling Better, Getting Better, Staying Better* (Atascadero, California: Impact Publishers, 2001).

—— *The Myth of Self-Esteem* (Amherst, N.Y.: Prometheus Books, 2006).

EMERSON, RALPH WALDO, "Self-Reliance", from *Essays: First Series* (1841).

FERDOWSI, *The Epic of Kings: Shah-Nama*, trans. Reuben Levy (Abingdon, Oxon: Routledge, 2011).

FRANKL, VIKTOR EMIL, *Man's Search for Meaning* (first published in German in 1946; London: Ebury Press, 2004).

FROMM, ERICH, *The Art of Being* (New York: Continuum, 1992).

—— *The Art of Loving* (Thorsons edn; London: HarperCollins, 1995).

GANDHI, MAHATMA, *Gandhi: All Men Are Brothers*, ed. Krishna Kripalani (New York: Continuum, 2004).

—— *My Non-violence*, ed. Sailesh Kumar Bandopadhaya (Ahmedabad: Navajivan Pub. House, 1960).

—— *The Epic Fast* (1932); in *Gandhi: All Men Are Brothers*, ed. Krishna Kripalani (New York: Continuum International Publishing Group, 2004).

GEERTZ, CLIFFORD, "Thick Description: Toward an Interpretive Theory of Culture", paraphrasing the sociologist Max Weber; in Clifford Geertz (ed.), *The Interpretation of Cultures* (New York: Basic Books, 1973).

GOETHE, JOHANN WOLFGANG VON, *Goethe's Opinions on the World, Mankind, Literature, Science, and Art*, trans. Otto Wenckstern (London: John W. Parker & Son, 1853).

GRACIÁN, BALTASAR, *Art of Worldly Wisdom*, trans. Joseph Jacobs (Whitefish, Montana: Kessinger Publishing, 2003).

HAIDT, JONATHAN, *The Happiness Hypothesis: Putting Ancient Wisdom and Philosophy to the Test of Modern Science* (London: Arrow Books, 2006).

HANSEN, C., "Classical Chinese Ethics"; in P. Singer (ed.), *A Companion to Ethics* (Oxford: Basil Blackwell, 1991).

HESCHEL, ABRAHAM J., *The Insecurity of Freedom: Essays on Human Existence* (New York: Farrar, Straus & Giroux, 1967).

HILLEL, RABBI, *Talmud Bavli* [*Babylonian Talmud*], Tractate

Shabbos, Schottenstein edition, trans. A. Dicker
(New York: Mesorah Publications, 1996).

HILTEBEITEL, ALF, *Dharma: Its Early History in Law,
Religion, and Narrative* (New York: Oxford
University Press, 2011).

IYENGAR, B. K. S., *Astadala Yogamala*, Vol. 2
(New Delhi: Allied Publishers, 2001).

JOBS, STEVE, "Steve Jobs: How to live before you die",
Stanford University commencement speech
(12 June 2005), posted December 2009.
<http://www.ted.com/talks/steve_jobs_how_to_
live_before_you_ die.html>. Accessed 6 October
2011.

JUNG, CARL GUSTAV, *Memories, Dreams, Reflections*
(New York: Vintage Books, 1989).

KAVIRAJA GOSWAMI, SHRILA KRISHNADASA, *Shri
Caitanya-caritamrita* (with commentaries by
Shrila Bhaktivinoda Thakura and Shrila
Bhaktisiddhanta Sarasvati Goswami Thakura)
(Kolkata: Gaudiya Matha, 1958).

KOCKELMANS, JOSEPH J., Edmund Husserl's
Phenomenology (West Lafayette, Indiana: Purdue
University Press, 1994).

LA ROCHEFOUCAULD, *Collected Maxims and Other
Reflections*, trans. E. H. Blackmore and A. M.
Blackmore (Oxford, New York: Oxford University
Press, 2008).

LAWRENCE, D. H., "Cypresses"; in D. H. Lawrence,
The Complete Poems of D.H. Lawrence (Ware,
Hertfordshire: Wordsworth Editions, 1994).

LEYS, S. (ed.), *The Analects of Confucius* (New York: Norton, 1997).

MACHIAVELLI, NICCOLÒ, *The Prince and the Discourses* (first published in 1532), trans. L. Ricci and C . E. Detmold (New York: Modern Library, 1940).

MAHARAJ, NISARGADATTA and ROBERT POWELL, *The Nectar of Immortality: Sri Nisargadatta Maharaj's Discourses on the Eternal*, ed. by Robert Powell (Delhi: Motilal Banarsidass, 2004).

MALINAR, ANGELIKA, *The Bhagavadgita: Doctrines and Contexts* (Cambridge: Cambridge University Press, 2007).

"Manager's Best Friend: Dogs Improve Office Productivity", The Economist [website] (12 August 2010). <http://www.economist.com/node/16789216?story_id=16789216>. Accessed 22 August 2010.

MASCARO, J. (ed. and trans.), *The Dhammapada* (Harmondsworth, England: Penguin, 1973).

MCADAMS, DAN P., "Can Personality Change? Levels of Stability and Growth in Personality Across the Life Span", in T. F. Heatherton and J. L. Weinberger (eds.), *Can Personality Change?* (Washington, DC: American Psychological Association, 1994).

MEHENDALE, M. A., *"Satyam eva jayate nanritam"*, *Journal of the American Oriental Society*, Vol. 81 (1961), pp. 405–8.

MEHROTRA, RAJA RAM, "Verbalization of Polite Behaviour in Indian English", in *The Third International Symposium on Language and*

Linguistics (Bangkok, Thailand: Chulalongkorn University, 1992).

MILLS, MARY, "Propaganda and Children during the Hitler Years" (The Nizkor Project). <http://www.nizkor.org/hweb/people/m/mills-mary/mills-00.html>. Accessed 13 November 2011.

MONIER-WILLIAMS, MONIER, *A Sanskrit-English Dictionary* (Oxford, Clarendon Press, 1964).

MÜLLER, FRIEDRICH MAX, *The Satapatha-Brahmana, Madhyandina School*, Vol. 12., Part I, Books 1 and 2 (Clarendon Press, 1882; reprint by Motilal Banarsidass, 1972).

NARAYANA MAHARAJA, SHRI SHRIMAD BHAKTIVEDANTA, *Shri Brahma-samhita* (with commentaries of Shrila Jiva Goswami, Shrila Bhaktivinoda Thakura and Shri Shrimad Bhaktivedanta Narayana Maharaja) (Vrindavan, India: Gaudiya Vedanta Publications, 2003).

—— *Shri Gaudiya Giti-guccha* (Vrindavan, India: Gaudiya Vedanta Publications, 2003).

—— *Shrimad Bhagavad-gita* (with *bhavanuvada* of the commentary of Shrila Vishvanatha Chakravarti Thakura and commentary by Shri Shrimad Bhaktivedanta Narayana Maharaja) (Vrindavan, India: Shri Gaudiya Vedanta Samiti, 2000).

NARAYANA PANDITA, SHRI and FRIEDRICH MAX MÜLLER, *The First Book of the Hitopadesha: Containing the Sanskrit Text, with Interlinear Transliteration, Grammatical Analysis, and English Translation*

(London: Longman, Green, Longman, Roberts, & Green, 1864).

—— *The Second, Third, and Fourth Books of the Hitopadesha: Containing the Sanskrit Text, with Interlinear Translation* (London: Longman, Green, Longman, Roberts, & Green, 1865).

New Revised Standard Bible (1989), BibleStudyTools. com [website]. <http://www.biblestudytools. com/nrs/>. Accessed 29 November 2012.

NIETZSCHE, FRIEDRICH, *Beyond Good and Evil: Prelude to a Philosophy of the Future*, trans. Walter Kaufmann (New York: Vintage, 1989).

PODGER, CORINNE, "Quarter of Mammals 'Face Extinction'", BBC News [website], 21 May 2002. <http://news.bbc.co.uk/1/hi/sci/tech/2000325.stm>. Accessed 18 December 2007.

POLO, MARCO, *The Travels of Marco Polo, a Venetian, in the Thirteenth Century*, trans. William Marsden (London: William Marsden, 1818).

PROUST, MARCEL, *In Search of Lost Time,* Vol. 2, *Within a Budding Grove*, trans. C. K. S. Moncreiff and T. Kilmartin (London: Chatto and Windus, 1992).

—— *Remembrance of Things Past*, Vol. 3, trans. C. K. Scott Moncrieff and Terence Kilmartin (New York: Vintage Books, 1982).

REYNA, RUTH, *Introduction to Indian Philosophy* (New Delhi: Tata McGraw-Hill Publishing, 1964).

RUMI, JALAL AL-DIN, and COLEMAN BARKS et al.,
The Essential Rumi (New York: HarperCollins,
1995; new expanded edn, 2004).

RUPA GOSWAMI, SHRILA, *Shri Bhakti-rasamrita-sindhu*
(with commentaries by Shrila Jiva Goswami, Shri
Mukunda Goswami and Shrila Vishvanatha
Chakravarti Thakura), Sanskrit to Bengali trans.
Haridasa Dasa (Navadwip, India: Haribol Kutir,
1945).

—— *Shri Bhakti-rasamrita-sindhu* (with commentary by
Shrila Jiva Goswami) (Varanasi: Acyuta Granthamala
Series, 1977).

—— *Shri Bhakti-rasamrita-sindhu* (with commentary by
Shrila Jiva Goswami), Sanskrit to Bengali trans.
Kanailala Adhikari and Bankima Chandra
Panda (Mayapur, India: Shri Chaitanya Gaudiya
Matha, 2001).

—— *Shri Upadeshamrita* (with commentaries by Shri
Radha-Ramana Goswami, Shrila Bhaktivinoda
Thakura and Shrila Bhaktisiddhanta Sarasvati
Goswami Thakura), Sanskrit to Bengali trans.
Shri Shrimad Bhakti-dayita Madhava Maharaja
(Navadwip, India: Shri Chaitanya Gaudiya Matha,
1981).

—— *Shri Upadeshamrita* (with commentaries by Shri
Radha-Ramana Goswami, Shrila Bhaktivinoda
Thakura and Shrila Bhaktisiddhanta Sarasvati
Goswami Thakura), from Hindi trans. of Shri
Shrimad Bhaktivedanta Narayana Maharaja

(Vrindavan, India: Gaudiya Vedanta Publications, 2003).

SANATANA GOSWAMI, SHRILA, and SHRILA GOPALA BHATTA GOSWAMI, *Shri Hari-bhakti-vilasa* (with "Dig-darshini-tika" by Shrila Sanatana Goswami), Sanskrit to Bengali trans. Maha-nama-vrata Brahmachari (Kolkata: Mahesh Library, 1993).

SARASVATI GOSWAMI THAKURA, SHRILA BHAKTISIDDHANTA, *Shri Brahma-samhita* (Madras: Tridandi Shri Bhakti Prajnana Yati, 1973).

SCHRÖDINGER, ERWIN, *Nature and the Greeks* (London: Cambridge University Press, 1954).

SELIGMAN, M. E. P., T. A. STEEN, N. PARK and C. PETERSON, "Positive Psychology Progress: Empirical Validation of Interventions", *American Psychologist*, 60 (2005), pp. 410–421.

SHAKESPEARE, WILLIAM, *The Oxford Shakespeare: The Complete Works*, second edition, ed. Stanley Wells, Gary Taylor, John Jowett and William Montgomery (Oxford: Oxford University Press, 2005).

SHASTRI, J. I. (ed.), *Manusmriti with the Sanskrit Commentary Manvarthamuktavali of Kulluka Bhatta* (New Delhi: Motilal Banarsidass, 1990).

SHRIDHARA MAHARAJA, SHRILA B. R., "The Panacea", *Rays of The Harmonist*, No.11 (Karttika, 2002).

SHRIDHARA SWAMI, SHRILA, *Subodhini-tika* (Kolkata: Gaudiya Mission, 1946).

SHRIDHARA SWAMI, SHRILA, SHRI VAMSHIDHARA, SHRI RADHA-RAMANA GOSWAMI, SHRI VIRA-RAGHAVACHARYA

et al., *Shrimad-Bhagavatam*, Canto 1 (with the
Sanskrit commentaries of Shrila Shridhara Swami
["Bhavartha-dipika"], Shri Vamshidhara ["Bhavartha-
dipika-prakasha"], Shri Radha-Ramana Goswami
["Dipani"], Shri Vira-Raghavacharya ["Bhagavata-
chandrika"], Shri VijayadhvajaTirtha ["Pada-ratnavali"],
Shrila Jiva Goswami ["Krama-sandarbha"], Shrila
Vishvanatha Chakravarti Thakura ["Sarartha-darshini"],
Shri Shukadeva Acharya ["Siddhanta-pradipa"], Shri
Vallabhacharya ["Subodhini"], Shri Purushottama-
charana Goswami ["Subodhini-prakasha"] and Shri
Giridhara Lala Goswami ["Bala-prabodhini"]),
compiled by Krishna Shankara Shastri (Ahmedabad,
Krishna Shankara Shastri, 1965).

SIDDHANTI GOSWAMI, BHAKTI SHRI RUPA, et al., trans.,
Mundaka Upanishad (Kolkata: Sarasvata Gaudiya
Mission, 1971).

—— *Shrimad Bhagavad-gita with the Gita-bhushana
Commentary of Shrila Baladeva Vidyabhushana*
(Kolkata: Sarasvata Gaudiya Mission, 1967).

—— *Shvetashvatara Upanishad* (Kolkata: Sarasvata
Gaudiya Mission, 1971).

SPINNEY, LAURA, "All About Me", *New Scientist*, Vol. 214,
No. 2862 (28 April 2012), p. 44–47.

STEVENSON, ROBERT LOUIS, *Essays of Robert Louis
Stevenson*, ed. William Lyon Phelps (Rockville,
Maryland: Arc Manor, 2008).

"The Millionaire Tramp", *The New York Times*,
20 February 1886.

VALÉRY, PAUL, *Monsieur Teste*, trans. Jackson Mathews (A. A. Knopf, 1947).

VEDA-VYASA, KRISHNA DVAIPAYANA, *Brihadaranyakopanishad* (Gorakhapur, India: Gita Press).

—— *Chandogyopanishad* (Gorakhapur, India: Gita Press).

—— *Kenopanishad* (Gorakhapur, India: Gita Press).

—— *Mahabharata*, 6 vols, (Gorakhapur, India: Gita Press, 1942).

—— *Mundakopanishad* (Gorakhapur, India: Gita Press).

—— *Rig Veda Samhita*, ed. R. L. Kashyap and S. Sadagopan (Bangalore: Sri Aurobindo Kapali Sastry Institute of Vedic Culture, 1998).

—— *Skanda Purana* (Gorakhapur, India: Gita Press, 1951).

—— *Shrimad-Bhagavata Maha-puranam* (Gorakhapur, India: Gita Press).

—— *Shvetashvataropanishad* (Gorakhapur, India: Gita Press).

—— *Taittiriya Samhita*, ed. Vijayaraghavan Bashyam (Hyderabad: 2005). <http://www.sanskritweb.net/yajurveda/>. Accessed 29 November 2012.

—— *Taittiriyopanishad* (Gorakhapur, India: Gita Press).

VISHNU SHARMA, SHRI, *The Panchatantraka of Vishnusarman*, ed. Kashinatha Panduranga Paraba (Tukaram Javji, 1896).

VOWEL, CHELSEA, "Check the Tag on that 'Indian' Story" [blog post], 21 February 2011. <http://apihtawikosisan.com/2012/02/21/check-the -tag-on-that-indian-story/>. Accessed 23 April 2012.

WALTON, MARSHA, "Study: Only 10 Percent of Big Ocean Fish Remain", CNN [website], 14 May 2003. <http://www.cnn.com/2003/TECH/science/05/14/coolsc.disappearingfish/>. Accessed 18 December 2007.

WARE, BRONNIE, *The Top Five Regrets of the Dying: A Life Transformed by the Dearly Departing* (Bloomington, Indiana: Balboa Press, 2011).

WILDE, OSCAR, *Soul of Man under Socialism* (1891); published in Oscar Wilde, *Collected Works of Oscar Wilde* (Ware, Hertfordshire: Wordsworth Editions, 1997).

WILHELM, HELLMUT, and C. F. BAYNES, *The I Ching or Book of Changes* (Princeton, New Jersey: Princeton University Press, 1967).

WINTERNITZ, MORIZ, *A History of Indian Literature*, Vol. 1, trans. S. Ketkar (Calcutta: University of Calcutta, 1927).

WITTGENSTEIN, LUDWIG, *Culture and Value*, ed. G. H. von Wright, trans. Peter Winch (Chicago: University of Chicago Press, 1984).

—— *Philosophical Occasions*, ed. James C. Klagge and Alfred Nordmann (Indianapolis and Cambridge, Massachusetts: Hackett, 1993).

ACKNOWLEDGEMENTS

THIS BOOK WOULD NOT HAVE BEEN POSSIBLE without the support of many friends and well-wishers. I am especially thankful to Dr Michael Geary of Cranmore Foundation, who not only encouraged me to write about Dharma but also shared many of his insights on the subject. I am grateful also to Professor Bert Mulder, Lucy Lowsley-Williams and Hilde Mulder of Cranmore Foundation for our several discussions together about Dharma and on how to culturally translate the teachings of ancient India for contemporary Western readers.

My warm thanks to Ananta Moy, Vaijayanti Mala, David Haas and Crispian Mills for kindly looking over the manuscript at its various stages and offering valuable feedback. I am thankful to James Ellis-Brown for his help in reproducing the diagrams for this book, and to Radha

Blinderman for her help in translating some of the Sanskrit commentaries on the *Bhagavata Purana*. I am also deeply grateful to Pedro Catena for his design and layout of this book. He is a dear friend with a profound appreciation for the sacred teachings of India.

I am especially thankful to my wife, Mohini, for her unflagging support and extensive feedback, and for being a light of inspiration in my own spiritual journey.

Words are a paltry currency through which to express my indebtedness to my spiritual teacher, Shrila B. V. Narayan Goswami, who left this world on 29 December 2010. A living embodiment of wisdom, he was a father to me and showed me what it means to make life an expression of love. Through him, I learned a little about the extent of my own foolishness. I dedicate this book to him.

About the Author

Born in 1975, Simon Haas first became interested in the study of ancient wisdom traditions twenty-five years ago. As a boy, he began studying the Sanskrit texts of ancient India and lived for many years in temple monasteries in India. He apprenticed for sixteen years with an elderly master practitioner in the Bhakti tradition, within an unbroken line of teachers that dates back thousands of years.

Simon graduated with honours from the University of Cambridge. Currently, he focuses on making the teachings of ancient India accessible to contemporary readers and audiences. He lectures and gives seminars and workshops internationally on the philosophy of yoga and the ancient teachings of India.

www.bookofdharma.com
simon@bookofdharma.com